MEMOIRS AND MEDLEYS

THE AUTOBIOGRAPHY OF A
BOTTLE WASHER

Of Beauty I haven't a stock;
I believe I could startle a clock:
But - my face - I don't - mind it,
For I am behind it :—
The people in front - get - the shock

"Photoed by Archibald Gorrie.
The only unkindness I've known him to do"

MEMOIRS AND MEDLEYS
THE AUTOBIOGRAPHY OF A BOTTLE WASHER

TOM BARCLAY
(1852–1933)

COALVILLE PUBLISHING COMPANY
1995

First Published: 1934 by Edgar Backus, 44/46 Cank Street, Leicester.

Acknowledgements: To those who by their financial support, either by sponsorship or by advance subscription, made the publication of this new edition possible.

New introductions: © 1995 Dr. David Nash

© 1995 Nessan Danaher, Irish Studies Workshop (Leicester).

Proofreading of new material: Lawrence Grady

Typesetting: Steve Duckworth at Coalville Publishing Co.

This edition published by Coalville Publishing Company Ltd. 1995

© 1995 Coalville Publishing Company Ltd.
The Springboard Centre, Mantle Lane, Coalville, Leicestershire, U.K.

ISBN 1 872478 30 8

Printed at Alden Press Limited, Oxford and Northampton, Great Britain.

CONTENTS

ILLUSTRATIONS

FOREWORD

OF the many good things that have come to me through my membership of the Leicester Secular Society not the least was the friendship of Tom Barclay. It began as far back as 1884 but my earliest definite recollection is of a delightful walk on Charnwood Forest in 1886 or 1887, when Tom and his friend Robson were walking and talking the whole day with my brother Ernest and me. Our object was not so much the walk as a discussion of Socialism and Individualism, Tom and Robson, Socialists ; Ernest and I, Individualists. Hyndman, William Morris and Bernard Shaw had recently lectured in the Secular Hall on the one side and Auberon Herbert, Wordsworth Donisthorpe and J. H. Levy on the other. We were all young, enthusiastic and much in earnest. I think we noticed little of the country, we were too deeply buried in the discussion. We had a lovely warm day and a warm but entirely friendly discussion, and the result was to make each of us more thoroughly convinced that our own philosophy was the most hopeful.

May I now, nearly fifty years after, confess that I think that Tom and Robson were nearer to the "Eternal Verities" than we were, though I still think that we all had our share. There was much of the best type of Individualism in Tom Barclay, as the following pages show.

From those days until his death on New Year's Day of 1933 Tom Barclay was a familiar figure in the

FOREWORD

Secular Club and Lecture Hall, active in the social
and intellectual life of the community. When the
seven lectures by young, but afterwards famous,
Fabians were given to us in 1888 and 1889 (afterwards
published as *Fabian Essays in Socialism*) Tom wrote
descriptive reports of them for Morris's *Commonwealth*. All through the years his deep musical voice,
with its touch of Irish brogue, was heard in the
discussions which followed lectures by Socialists,
Individualists, Freethinkers, Clergymen, Russian
Exiles and all sorts and conditions of men. Often
he would gently pull the lecturer's leg with an
apparently artless question which carried a deep
hidden meaning. He was always eager for any addition
to knowledge. Always gentle and courteous. He
would express indignation at any injustice but never
seemed to lose his temper, and for that reason was
always more effective.

At social gatherings he would sometimes sing a
delightful Irish song or give a jolly step dance. He
was all round first-rate company. He had no desire
for office and I don't think he was ever a member of
committee.

He was wonderfully gifted in many ways. He
sketched a number of self-portraits and caricatures to
which he attached humorous descriptions (one is
given in this book) which showed real power as an
artist. I believe his life was a happy one though it
makes one's blood boil to think of such a man living
under such hard conditions. Friends would have
been glad to make his last few years easier for him,
but he was too independent to accept help so long as

FOREWORD

he could scrape along. It hurt sometimes to see him in his very shabby old garments but he wore them with an unconscious dignity which carried a lesson for many of us.

Sydney A. Gimson

January 15th, 1934.

A Critical Introduction to Tom Barclay's *Memoirs and Medleys: The Autobiography of A Bottle Washer*

Tom Barclay, socialist intellectual proletarian and "bottle washer", displays in his autobiography and outlook a capacity for bitingly sharp insight along with a naïvety which brilliantly conjures up for us the life of the late nineteenth-century political and intellectual activist. Whilst Tom Barclay's individual character speaks genuinely to the modern reader, it is the range of influences that have created his world view that are of concern to the historian. In many respects this is the enduring value of autobiographies – that they show how individuals accept or reject ideas and how otherwise incompatible ideas can coexist alongside one another. In this respect such autobiographies can turn cultures which often exist only for the historian in the pages of dry texts into living responses to a variety of historical experiences and situations.

The function of these two introductions is to emphasise the importance of such influences and to indicate why the range of them makes Tom Barclay's *Memoirs and Medleys* a unique document for the study of the Irish diaspora in England, of nineteenth-century secularism, of socialism and of the culture of self-learning. *Memoirs and Medleys* evokes compelling pictures of the poverty of his early life in the mid-Victorian period, of his religious upbringing and the revolt from this which made him a secularist. It analyses his developing socialism and lastly reflects upon the autodidactism which underpinned it all.

In the midst of Edward Thompson's description in *William Morris: Romantic to Revolutionary* of how working men took to the ideas of William Morris, the author describes the enthusiasm generated in the provinces by men like Tom Barclay:

> He devoured every book that came his way, he bought or begged a pencil and became a talented draughtsman – a scholar, a writer and a Socialist .... the Socialist propaganda

brought such people as these exactly what it had brought to William Morris – hope. Wherever the aspiration for life stirred among the workers – the clear headed hatred of capitalism, the thirst for knowledge, beauty and fellowship – the Socialist converts might be won. Such converts might seem "oddities", it is true: but it is by such "oddities" as these that history is made.[1]

At first sight the picture of an intense Irishness in exile stands in stark contrast to Thompson's argument about Barclay as a paragon of that most English form of radicalism – Morrisite Socialism. However, this is to misunderstand the complex pressures that competing ideologies exerted on radicals in the 1880s. Perhaps some aspects of this irony are accommodated in Sydney Gimson's recognition in the original foreword to this book that despite his avowed socialism "there was much of the best type of individualism in Tom Barclay".[2]

Barclay's picture of his own childhood is genuinely harrowing, with his early life stalked by fear, disease and poverty. This is a common thread which runs through many nineteenth-century working-class autobiographies and it emphasises the effect of poverty on all areas of working-class family relations. As one historian has put it "the home was not seen as a refuge but a cockpit, the arena in which the consequences of exploitation and inequality were experienced and battled with".[3] Barclay describes various early homes in Leicester as a "pigsty-crib" or "a dirty kennel" perpetually infested with a mixture of bugs, lice and black beetles. Hunger was felt keenly in this environment and his account of offering his tongue to his siblings as a substitute for the mother's nipple is a vivid illustration that has a profound effect on modern readers. This sort of formative experience in the life of 19th-century radicals is well catalogued.[4]

Barclay's mother is portrayed as a hardy woman, able to do without a midwife, who consoled herself with Irish lamentations or meditations upon the suffering of "Our Blessed Lord". The liking of his father for strong drink is depicted as an acute domestic problem, one of Vincent's "consequences of inequality", but Barclay's obvious sympathy for both his father and mother comes very close to analysing the problem. Whilst his father becomes an object of pity, driven to the alehouse by the pain of poverty and want, his mother's ability to carry on provokes Barclay to note poignantly that it is women who are both the economic and psychological managers of poverty.

Thus it is not surprising that Barclay had no time for those who criticised the alleged immorality of the poor and their apparent addiction to drink. The judgement that this addiction was due to the moral failings of a whole class was prevalent amongst many who administered the official and unofficial organs of welfare within late Victorian England. In particular the Charity Organisation Society, which had a strong presence in Leicester, based its programme on helping those who appeared capable of helping themselves whilst deliberately choosing to neglect those who were perceived to be beyond help. Even within sections of Leicester socialism and secularism, there were those like the somewhat puritanical City Councillor and Secular Society organiser F.J. Gould, who blamed the debasement of the working class and their lack of enthusiasm for programmes of reform upon the corrosive power of alcohol. Barclay's reply was to point out how destitution and grinding poverty drove those who suffered from them to take what solace they could in drink. Thus Barclay's journalistic venture into the Northgate Street area produced an almost classical social investigative exposé of the housing conditions and the degenerate morning habits of the local women. However, this subtle use of an established mode of writing is twisted by Barclay in the final sentence when he reminds readers that:

> We can't be too careful in ascertaining whether a desire to drink is the cause of the slum or whether the slum is the cause of the desire to drink.

However, Barclay went further. The following edition of the paper contained his invented reply from the women he had written about. The piece paints a picture of a vibrant and mutually supportive community which the orthodox social investigator would miss. The women are portrayed as cheering each other through misfortune and keeping alive some semblance of simple recreation in the face of the demands of home and family while the men enjoy the burgeoning opportunities offered by professional sport and the Music Hall. This aspect in its way echoes Barclay's conviction that poverty and middle class reforming attitudes to morality single working-class women out for particularly harsh treatment.

While Tom Barclay rails against the material poverty suffered by the people of his class his account of childhood identifies an equally keenly felt destitution. The boredom and lack of mental stimulation caused by poverty is something that social commentators, then as now, so easily overlook. As such, Barclay's picture of himself as a child begging for a pencil and later as a young man trying to master the intricacies of a vocabulary that was alien to those around him is especially poignant.

Throughout his autobiography Tom Barclay reasserts a confidence in the power and value of intellect, promoting it through all the channels that were available to him. This was an outlook based upon his own experience that, whilst constrained by the poverty of material conditions, the power represented by intellect embodied the most viable form of freedom available to "the intellectual proletaire". The desire and ability to use the fruits of learning to transcend class limitations whilst maintaining a life-style and attitude which carried lifelong poverty as a badge has been described by one historian as a culture of poverty.[5] The essence of this culture was the notion of struggle often tempered by a tendency to fatalistic views of life and an addiction to immediate gratification. Whilst it was essential to deplore the fact of the struggle for the necessities of life – food, housing, employment and education – the outlook of a man like Tom Barclay turned this struggle into a virtue. Contained within this struggle for knowledge was the idea that such knowledge was better appreciated because it had been hard won. Moreover this had the virtue of putting individuals more in control of their own education than they would be in a conventional curriculum. Though this attitude may appear stubborn, insular and short-sighted to the modern reader it is easy to forget that the twentieth century is an age of state education and considerably wider educational opportunities. For Barclay and others like him the opening of a Free Library, which prompted him to dust off his Sunday-best suit for his first visit, represented the highest level of educational provision he could expect access to.[6]

The experience of maintaining and then losing his Catholic faith in a foreign country had a profound effect upon Tom Barclay and this is intimated in *Memoirs and Medleys*. In some respects his experience of this is exceptional, since the cohesive nature of Irish immigrant communities acted as a link for many with their homeland and their Catholic upbringing. However it is almost certainly true that, like the rest of Victorian society, those who rejected Christianity are less apparent to the historian and as a result have been comparatively neglected. Thus Tom Barclay's account of losing his faith is a valuable pointer to the untold experience of many others. What makes this account distinctive is the fact that this was a positive rejection of Catholicism and Christianity, rather than a drifting away from the traditional community ties and the resultant dilution of belief and observance that was common to the Irish "lapsers", who found themselves marginalised from their communities by a volatile labour market.

Early in life Tom noticed a number of inconsistencies with the religion of his family. His enjoyment of alcohol was increasingly difficult to square with the notion of confession and his experience of others who expressed devout belief alongside precocious sexual knowledge taught him the meaning of hypocrisy. [7] Despite this, Barclay initially remained a fierce defender of his beliefs by adopting St Thomas Aquinas as his patron saint. However it was the struggle of defending his beliefs that eventually led to a recognition that "All the thought and fact and evidence seemed to be on the side of the sceptic and unbeliever".[8] Traces of these thoughts litter *Memoirs and Medleys* – the question of why God can allow devils free rein on earth and the portrayal of a Dominican sermon on the torments of Hell comparable to that in Joyce's *Portrait of the Artist as a Young Man* both indicate formative experiences in the rejection of religion. The dichotomy between faith and human fallibility is given a comic tinge in his suggestion that he found turning to the Douay bible stirred up in him erotic thoughts when he previously shunned Protestant bibles for this very reason. Despite these obvious problems with retaining the Catholic faith, one aspect seems to stand out as paramount in Tom Barclay's apostasy – the implicit denial of reason and intellect that it clearly contained:

Why have an intelligence if one cannot trust it? I am just as sincere now that I believe in no creed as I was at the time of the Mission, and at that time I was transfigured.[9]

From the position of sceptic Tom Barclay became a seeker visiting Mormons, Christadelphians, Brahmins and Buddhists before reaching a final resting place within the doctrine of secularism which laid firm and lasting roots in late Victorian Leicester.[10] Secularism had first surfaced nationally in the 1850s as a means of organising and defending those who rejected Christian belief. One reason for its success in Leicester was its appeal to artisan values of self-education and self-improvement which flourished in a locality which had yet to suffer the de-skilling of its major industries that was progressing apace elsewhere. Though not an artisan in the conventional sense Tom Barclay exemplifies this process in action – the rejection of

Christianity within a hostile world together with his commitment to intellectual achievement indicate why he was attracted to secularism. During his membership of the Leicester Secular Society Tom never became a member of its numerous committees; indeed the minutes refer to him as an "irregular member" since he had difficulty finding the subscription fee. However this short-sighted, rather bourgeois judgement misses the fact that Barclay's ideological and intellectual involvement was greatly valued and the foreword to *Memoirs and Medleys* by the Society's president, Sydney Ansell Gimson, provides evidence of this.

Memoirs and Medleys not only provides us with one of the insights into life in the Leicester Secular Society but it is also a valuable record of grassroots thought and opinion amongst this often forgotten and overlooked movement that has national relevance. Thus Barclay's conversion experience is outlined alongside his latterday criticisms of his former faith. Interestingly enough, Tom took most of his secularist inspiration more from the writings of the American, Robert Ingersoll, than from the established English secular ideologues Charles Bradlaugh, John Mackinnon Robertson or George William Foote. Alongside his consumption of these texts and the serious free thought newspapers Tom Barclay also read the far more irreverent *Freethinker*, which contained cartoons and comic representations of biblical incidents and religious doctrines. He mentions his own great amusement at a particular cartoon which portrays Christ's attempt to walk on water as aided by a canoe under each foot. Similarly he howled with laughter at the physical implausibilities of foddering the animals during the deluge.[11] This is an important reminder that humour was a particularly cogent weapon in the armoury of the individual freethinker and as popular images such cartoons could be used by freethinkers to say more than the most painstakingly constructed argument was able to do.

It is clear from *Memoirs and Medleys* that Tom Barclay was happiest as a freethinker and during the course of the book he makes the very important point that those who chided him for losing his faith assumed rashly that it was a backsliding and easy choice for him to make. This view neglects the torment that he suffered during his renunciation of the faith. Ultimately, as he says, it was the notion of Hell which was "the rock on which I split". He casts scorn on Aquinas for saying that the torments of the damned will intensify the bliss of the saved, preferring the secularist poet James Thomson's desire to be damned if damnation likewise embraces his fellow man. Freed from such religious ties Tom was eventually able, towards the end of his life, to put the notion of religious belief into a kinder perspective.

> I look at all religions as attempts to explain the Mystery of Being – the meaning of Life – why we're here, and what we ought to do, and what's going to become of us – the meaning of it all.[12]

Tom Barclay's politicisation can be read as one that would have been common to many during this period who might be called old radicals. The lectures and speeches he heard from G.J. Holyoake and Thomas Cooper provide a link with early century radicalism. An interest in political economy after reading the works of Adam Smith and John Stuart Mill was followed by an encounter with the land nationalisation schemes of Henry George.[13] Barclay was led from this to the ideas of John Ruskin through his manifesto *Unto this Last*. Eventually he felt himself so in tune with Ruskin's ideas that he issued a local cheap edition of extracts from it.[14] This was done in the fervent belief that individuals should be educated in progressive ideas if social and political change was to take place. Though radical, the ideas Barclay gleaned from Ruskin were not entirely in tune with a conventional socialist outlook. His early attacks were on rent and the simple facts of wealth amidst poverty. He asserted that riches were the robbery of labour, comparing the slums of Leicester's Denman and Metcalf streets with the villas of suburban Stoneygate. From this he argued for a moral decency, suggesting that, while servants were not required by the working classes, space and ventilation certainly were. Interestingly though, he maintains in the autobiography an enduring belief in meritocracy, suggesting that mansions, if they have to exist, should be distributed on social merit.

One aspect of this view which was important to Barclay was a conviction that a mere redistribution of wealth would not be enough. He saves much venom for working men who merely seek for material gain and attacks what he saw as simpleton proletarian economics, arguing that capitalism is not a way of life but a "Monte Carlo" in which larger capitalists invariably profit from the demise of smaller ones.[15] These attacks on the immorality of capitalism as a complete and total system were sharpened by Barclay's assimilation of the ideas of William Morris.

Barclay heard Morris lecture on Art and Socialism at the Leicester Secular Hall in January 1884 and this led him to become a founder member of the Leicester Branch of the Socialist League.[16] One important aspect of the Morrisite approach to socialism that Tom Barclay took to heart was the belief that socialists had to be consciously converted. It was this belief that led to his journalistic work, including *Countryman*, which he envisaged as a local equivalent of the Socialist League paper *Commonweal*. This approach was also behind Barclay's membership of numerous clubs and institutes, though he notes that he withdrew from them when they did not follow through the often-stated aim of becoming literary institutes.

Barclay's socialism also led him into activism in other spheres. He was a founder member of the Leicester Labour Club and was considerably influential in local trade union circles, having briefly occupied the post of general secretary of the Leicester Amalgamated Hosiery Union.[17] His involvement in these, however, was short-lived, possibly due to his unwillingness to oppose socialists with views different from his own. Indeed he thrived on a sort of eclecticism that would have been familiar to old radicals. He notes with pride that, at one time or another, he had belonged to the SDF, the Socialist League, the local

Anarchist Communist group and also the ILP, but was annoyed by each group's criticism of the other.[18] Though his work in these areas was important in the development of Leicester's labour movement, Tom Barclay's autobiography glosses over these events in favour of what could be described as his own personal culture of socialism.

Throughout *Memoirs and Medleys* there is an intense preoccupation with learning – its value, its processes, its acquisition and its ability to enrich the life of the individual. Again it is possible to find parallels with other self-taught writers. Barclay, however, shows a number of these attributes in abundance. Many incidents become an opportunity for him to display his widespread learning and an almost relentless name-dropping of authors and their works. These, he notes with a rare honesty, coexisted in his intellectual diet alongside penny literature. Also outlined is the classic obsession of the self-taught with grammar and with the gaining of certificates. Barclay even displays wisdom enough to paint a caricature of what it was like to be an autodidact who spent time reading instead of enjoying the sunshine:

> An old clothes-basket of books is pulled over towards the chamber window – second-hand, often tattered books, picked up from stalls in the market: discarded school-books with copious notes telling of "filthy loves of the gods and goddesses".[19]

The resort to books and intellectual pursuits, as has been suggested, was a common thread that ran through the lives of numerous radicals and spanned the whole nineteenth century. Whilst Barclay used them to enrich his own life and that of others he saw that knowledge had its own political dimension and he scorned the commercial value that others placed on it. Like the Owenites and Chartists before him he recognised that knowledge was power. Ground down by poverty, the proletarian intellectual's only access to power was through the pursuit and understanding of such knowledge. Once grasped it was the duty of the individual to communicate the benefits of the hard won quest. In this area the range of his writing and the various different audience registers that Barclay reaches in his autobiography and his journalism is impressive. His ability to move effortlessly from the artful and skilled recreation of Victorian poverty to the learned Latin of theologians gives us an important picture of a culturally different world. Barclay was pledged to the preservation of these different worlds and their inherent variety, nursing a rather less than secret ambition to move effortlessly between them.

Like all utopias this one had its enemies. Though capitalism is seen by Barclay as evil, it was the moral, intellectual and spiritual degradation of mankind that it carried with it that he so despised. He saw greed, indifference and corrupt taste as the enemies of human development, while surveying the progress of mankind through the medium of popular song. At this point the three strands of his ideology – secularism, socialism and his reverence for the quality use of time and intellect – are entwined in a single observation. The comment that the music hall turns "Champagne Charlie" and "Burgundy Benjamin" had become the deities offered for public worship bore out his perpetual complaint that mankind could always be enslaved by avarice and ignorance.

In some respects Tom Barclay was surely more like his hero, George Bernard Shaw, than he realised. He possessed the eye of the outsider and indulged his own keen sense of justice in all his undertakings. Though sometimes pedantic and verbose he was an acute, by turns serious and witty, observer of a society with which he associated but to which he quite obviously did not fully belong. Nonetheless the communication of those observations enriched the lives of all who were lucky enough to have had contact with these two men.

References.

1 E.P.Thompson, *William Morris: Romantic to Revolutionary* (1977 edition) p.300.

2 *Memoirs and Medleys*, Foreword.

3   David Vincent, *Bread, Knowledge and Freedom: A Study of Nineteenth-Century Working Class Autobiography* (1981) p. 55

4   See for example P. Hollis (Ed.), *Class and Conflict in 19th Century England 1815-50* (1973) pp. 293-298 for an account of the trial of Richard Pilling as an earlier example of this. Pilling's defence contains a number of harrowing references to the destitute condition of his wife and family, which was instrumental in driving him to political agitation. Likewise the accounts of Willie Thom (1844) and Henry Edward Price (1904) from Vincent (1981) pp.52-55 also make similarly grim reading. These examples indicate that material conditions for the immigrant populations of urban areas had not improved beyond those of impoverished native unskilled workers of twenty years earlier.

5   J.B. Haynes, "Working class perceptions: aspects of the experience of working-class life in Victorian Leicester." *Transactions of the Leicester Archaeological and Historical Society*, LXIII (1989) pp. 71-83.

6   *Memoirs and Medleys*, pp. 15 and 40.

7   *ibid* pp. 18 and 29.

8   *ibid* p. 44.

9   *ibid* pp. 18, 29, 30 and 31.

10   For a detailed discussion of Leicester secularism see D.S. Nash, *Secularism, Art and Freedom* (Leicester University Press 1992)

11   *Memoirs and Medleys*, pp. 48 and 52.

12   *ibid* p. 65-66.

13   *ibid* p. 46.

14   Tom Barclay, *The Rights of Labour According to John Ruskin* (Leicester, no date).

15   *Memoirs and Medleys*, p. 70.

16   See D.S. Nash, *Secularism, Art and Freedom* (Leicester University Press 1992) pp. 145-188 for a lengthy discussion of the full impact of the Morris visit on Leicester Secularism. See also Bill Lancaster, *Radicalism, Co-operation and Socialism* (Leicester University Press 1987) pp. 60-61.

17   See Lancaster pp. 22 and 114.

18   *Memoirs and Medleys*, p. 8.

19   *ibid* p. 19.

TOM BARCLAY THE IRISHMAN

A 1963 reminiscence of Tom Barclay paid him a deserved tribute "as one of Leicester's most remarkable citizens and a wholly lovable man"; briefly recalled were Barclay's Irish ancestry, and the fact that on his gravestone (still extant) part of the inscription reads, simply, "An Irishman."[1]

The local paper gave rather more clues to Barclay's contribution in his obituary notice thirty years earlier in 1933. Remarking that "many of the older generation of Leicester politicians and students will mourn the passing of Tom Barclay .... he was in humble circumstances all his life, yet he had more influence upon the city's intellectual life than most of those in high stations", the article went on to stress that "he was an Irishman – and proud of it – and his family came to Leicester not long after the famine years – 1846 and 1847."[2] It is interesting to note that, whilst many first and second generation Irish achievers are today "hijacked" by the British media as "English" celebrities (for example, Seamus Heaney), a provincial paper of earlier decades was quite comfortable with the notion of labelling Barclay with his parental ethnic background.

Barclay's role as an idealogue, idealist, socialist and secularist are dealt with in detail in the other part of this introduction: here, the focus is on his Irishness, and how, when and where he manifested this throughout his long life. Only in retrospect can the significance of Barclay's contribution to contemporary British-Irish debates be fully appreciated. He managed to deal honestly and thoroughly with many of the well-known and vexed issues of history, politics and religion; more important perhaps, was his ability to perceive, analyse and cogently present the then rarely-heard viewpoint of the second generation Irish in Britain. Barclay was before his time in articulating lucidly on key aspects of social and psychological issues of ethnic group identity; much of what he had to say, about Irish relations, Irish culture, and the Irish in Britain, has relevance today.

The fascination of the Irish dimensions of *Memoirs and Medleys* partly lies in the paradoxes that the author's experience presents to today's observer. These apparent contradictions are central to an understanding of the contemporary experience of the Irish in Britain:

- Barclay's ability to coalesce an Irish identity with a genuinely cosmopolitan outlook

- his development of an Irish identity without the assumed necessity of a Roman Catholic profile

- his willingness to tolerate positively all religious creeds whilst being a convinced atheist himself

- his capacity for balancing a radical leftist general outlook with a contrastingly moderate stance on Irish nationalism

- his commitment and enthusiasm for the Irish language and its revival, which co-existed with a blunt appreciation of the fact that to be and feel Irish did *not* necessarily involve the concomitant ideal of being able to understand and use Gaelic.

To fully appreciate Barclay's contribution, it is necessary to look briefly at the Leicester that he was born into in 1852. It was a typical provincial city and county town of the Victorian era, and one which had a sustained and prolonged exposure to controversial religious and political events affecting both Irish, and Roman Catholic, affairs. It is instructive to consider briefly two factors: the local Protestant tradition, and the collective local memory resulting from the experiences of Leicestershire soldiery vis-à-vis their long-term role in countering Irish disturbance and insurgency. [3]

The strong local inheritance of Protestantism stretched in an almost unbroken pattern from the pre-Reformation heretical sect of John Wycliffe's Lollards, through to the seventeenth century Puritan tradition, with local input from famed preachers with Irish connections such as John Howe and George Fox; it continued by embracing the antagonistic debates surrounding

Catholic Emancipation and the restoration of the Catholic hierarchy in 1829 and 1850 respectively. Barclay was born into a local community which, less than twenty years previously, had boasted two Orange Lodges, and whose partisan press together with the protestant churches maintained a steady antagonism towards any amelioration of Catholic conditions. The practice of inviting anti-Romanist preachers to the town never quite died out. Alessandro Gavazzi the renegade priest, John Kensit of militant Merseyside street evangelism, and much later the Rev. Ian Paisley, have all graced Leicester pulpits. As well as preacher-agitators, various anti-Romanist associations, patronised and supported by local aristocracy, gentry and clergy, existed across most of the mid- and later nineteenth century in Leicestershire. In general, in the nineteenth century in Leicester, Anglicanism was, on the whole, outright in its opposition to Roman Catholic growth; Non-conformist attitudes, however, varied, from a tolerant pluralist approach, to a more bitter and campaigning anti-papist stance.[4] Barclay mentions the prejudices, ethnic and religious, which he experienced at that time; quite possibly, his development as a secularist may in part and subconsciously have been influenced by the dominant, hostile protestant culture as well as the intellectual arguments presented through his self-education programme.

The other underlying factor that influenced the outlook of Leicester people towards Ireland in Barclay's time was the local reaction to what might be termed the repetitive rebellion syndrome. Research evidence indicates that Leicestershire soldiers (both in the Militia and the 17th Foot) had active experience of major Irish eruptions: not only did local men serve in Ireland from 1798, through until 1921 (and indeed beyond that date) on a very regular basis, they were active in putting down the 1798 Rising, the Easter Rebellion of 1916, and the Fenian invasion of Canada in the 1860's. Given these battle honours in the regimental records, and the coverage in local media of all these events, there must have been some local collective memory of the Irish as being a restless, troublesome set of people. Not surprisingly the Orange Lodges in the City in the 1830's were closely associated with the local military. Ironically, as Irish settlement in the town continued, significant numbers of Irish men served in the 17th Regiment – some being recruited in Ireland, others being second-generation Irish, born in Leicester, who had decided on military careers.[5]

In the light of these two local long-term trends, and the general background of negative attitudes based on religious, political and racial factors which attended Irish settlement in nineteenth century Britain, it is no surprise to find that Barclay was forced to articulate his response at a very young age.[6] Explaining exactly why he and his friends could not play freely in the street, he commented:

> Why had we to stay in? Well, you see, we might get lost or run over or beaten – hounded and ill used by the Sassenach kids: as a matter of fact we were hounded and harassed

> "Hurroo Mick!"

> "Ye Awrish Paddywack."

> "Arrah, bad luck to the ships that brought ye over!"

> These were the salutes from the happy English child: we were battered, threatened, elbowed, pressed back to the door of our kennel amid boos and jeers and showers of small missiles. The unkind expressions must have been borrowed from the grown-ups whose animosity was often evident enough.[7]

Recent oral history interviews confirm that anti-Catholic activities still occurred in Leicester and the Coalville area as late as the 1920's.

One could almost describe Barclay as a premature anti-racist. He conceded that most children, and indeed adults, of his time were ignorant in this respect for a variety of explicable reasons, and he pondered:

> I would like to know, and I wish I were anthropologist and psychologist enough to answer, is there any such reality as race-hatred? There should not be among intelligent grown-up people. My own attitude towards a foreigner of whatever colour or creed is simply one of interest – intense curiosity.[8]

That the prejudice was not one-sided he was prepared to explain; youthful street fights become subsumed in a culture clash:

> My imagination went to work: Billy was King William and we were the Irish: it was the siege of Limerick being in some mysterious manner enacted over again. There it was Gael and Sassenach once more.[9]

Barclay described at length his mother's judgement on the English and their historical traditions:

> Whenever an English man or woman did anything disreputable, my mother was wont to remark "Ah well, sure, what better could one expect from the breed of King Harry?" The Sassenach was regarded by us with a mixture of contempt and hatred. God had made him it is true and Jesus Christ had died to save him, but we clean forgot that, and only saw him embodied in Calvin and Cranmer, the lustful King Henry VIII, Queen Bess the Persecutor, the Orangeman's idol, William of Orange, and "The bloody Cromwell." There were though a few good Englishmen no doubt, like Alfred the Great, Sir Thomas More, and William Cobbett who wrote the history of the Protestant Reformation My father was a Limerick man, and we were often hearing eulogies of the hero Patrick Sarsfield, and the women of Limerick who fought and repelled the English during the siege of the city. How we gloated over the way the Irish Brigade defeated the English at Fontenoy![10]

Other more recent commentators have noted that many twentieth century Irish migrants coming to Britain brought with them a packaged nationalist history of Anglo-Irish relations similar to the one described by Barclay a century earlier.[11] Having noted this, it needs stating that the predominant "revisionist" thrust in modern Irish historiography has now extended itself into recent studies of the Irish in Britain, so that the simple model of victimized Irish enduring English misrule has been critically attacked for some decades. What is rather more problematical is getting historians to face up to the remaining contradictions, such as the inadequate and dishonest treatment of "the famine".[12] Even Barclay himself subscribed to the fatalist model: in the context of a description of his father, he remarked:

> You and mother and the rest of the wretched emigrants, victims of the 1848 potato blight, I often think of your condition – the sad exodus – penniless – trade-less – never to return to Erin! Did the famine-ships bring you over free? Brother was separated from brother – whole families broken up: one remained in Liverpool, one in the Potteries, and one went to America. Women as well as men tramped every foot of the road after leaving the boats: no trains for mere emigrants.[13]

Barclay was clearly ahead of his time in terms of his recognition of the role and importance of women. As the quotation above shows he was sensitively conscious of their role; in particular he explains in depth the social, economic and cultural responsibilities shouldered by his own mother.

Of most importance here perhaps is his mother's cultural role within the Irish migrant community:

> Mother taught me to spell and read. She was held to be quite exceptional among her countrywomen in that she could read Dr Gallacher's sermons in Irish. This Gallacher was the bishop of Raphoe in Donegal. How she who read English with difficulty could read these sermons, though in Roman characters, with their transliteration nearly as bad as Welsh, is something I do not understand: but read them she could, and often have I seen the tears come into her eyes

over the sermon on the passion of Our Lord. This she used
to read on Good Friday. "Glory to God but you're the one!"
neighbours used to exclaim. It did them good to hear a
blessed sermon read in the first language they ever spoke ...
She was well acquainted with the old legends of Oisin and
Fin, and Cuchullan, and the Gobawn Sayr, and could sing
and recite a goodly number of old Irish songs and poems.[14]

What is clear from this reasoned tribute is the four-fold
significance of his mother's role:

- the reinforcement provided for a minority religion in a
mode comprehensible to listeners.

- the sustenance of Gaelic, a minority language, in relatively
hostile surroundings.

- a community leadership function, involving the neighbours, and especially other women.

- the maintenance of the oral tradition in terms of folklore,
and in addition the transmission of historical information.

Barclay also commented on his father's literary tastes in reading
matter:

He had read Byron and Burns and Tom Moore, but I often
wonder how he acquired some twenty numbers of a
periodical called *The Celt*; he always pronounced the name
"Selt"; it was a Young Irelander periodical I believe.[15]

Elsewhere he indicates the development of his political consciousness, at a time when he would have been in his late teens:

Fenianism is rife about this time: I remember our parents
rejoicing over the escape from prison of— the Head Centre,
James Stephens (I think it was). Also, we were greatly
excited by the news of the blowing up of Clerkenwell
Prison. We lamented the hanging of the Manchester Martyrs,
and our English neighbours danced and rejoiced. What

wonder? Some priest said hell was not hot enough for the Fenians.[16]

Perhaps the hostility to the Fenians exhibited by the Roman Catholic Church, in Britain as well as in Ireland, hastened Barclay's progress to secularism. Bishop Ullathorne, of the neighbouring Roman Catholic diocese of Birmingham, made clear the Church's inimical views on these political issues, and registered serious concern at the growth and spread of Fenianism amongst the Irish in Britain.[17] Indeed, cutlasses and pistols were issued to the Leicester City Constabulary in 1867 at the height of the Fenian scare, even though Leicester was not involved directly in developments, local press hysteria notwithstanding.[18]

Barclay himself appears to have been a constitutional Irish nationalist, but curiously there is very little about the Home Rule campaign in his autobiography. He mentioned the existence of an Irish National Club;[19] it is only elsewhere that clues to his attitudes to Irish politics in the 1870's and 1880's can be found. A letter of Barclay's to the local press in 1882 concerning the Phoenix Park assassinations in Dublin was headed "Protest of an Irishman in Leicester". Barclay commented on the "cowardly and brutal murders", and claiming to speak for the Leicester Irish community, he spoke of "the greatest abhorrence" felt by all, and stated that the incidents would "make Irishmen hang down their heads."

This irrational assumption of self-guilt on the shoulders of the Irish in Britain is unusual for Barclay (it is similar to some of the views expressed by Irish community associations in Britain after the Warrington bombings of 1993); he was being more rational when he commented further on in the letter that the incident "would have created a prejudice against Irishmen and the Irish causes that will not easily be dissipated."[20]

The editor of the original memoir, James K. Kelly, quoted selections from Barclay's diaries in the epilogue chapter referring to the Irish liberation struggle earlier this century.

It would seem that in the period from 1916 to the end of the War of Independence, in 1921, Barclay desperately "wanted to *do* something – within three years of being sixty-seven – for poor, distracted, ill-fated Ireland." With regard to the post-Treaty period of civil war, Barclay noted despairingly:

> Beginning to be ashamed and disgusted with things Irish. Killing one another! Treatyite, Republican, Orangeman phut! Shades of Michael Davitt, Emmett, Tone, O'Connell, MacSweeny, Connolly, Orr, Tandy, Mitchell, Parnell, Davis, Smith O'Brien, Redmond, Sarsfield, Red Hugh, Pearse, O'Meagher, Duffy – O woe is me, my torment! Factions, reactions, distractions and ... and finally – Fractions![21]

The aspiration to action of 1916 had turned to the eventual disillusionment of 1921-2.

In fact, Barclay was of course a pro-active individual, and in terms of expressing the Irish dimensions to his existence, he managed to achieve a great deal, especially on the cultural and linguistic fronts. When he was in his forties, he flowered in almost a classical sense of being Irish. He witnessed at first hand the Gaelic revival taking place under the auspices of Conradh na Gaeilge (The Gaelic League). An entire chapter is devoted to this story. Although Barclay claimed not to be writing a history of this development, he certainly sheds much light on its personalities, priorities and practices. In an eighteen month period, after he moved to London, he unfailingly attended Irish language and ceilidh dancing classes. His comments on the problems associated with learning Irish are still to be heard on the lips of language tutors today. He was privileged, as he remarked, to meet the great names of the Gaelic literary revival. Among these were William Patrick Ryan and Francis Fahey.

It is possible that these two may have inspired Barclay in his practical efforts to launch Irish language classes in Leicester. Ryan was the author of *The Irish Literary Revival: Its History, Pioneers and Possibilities* (1894) which focused mainly on developments in Britain and which was virtually a directory of all the regional Irish cultural activity programmes going onat that time. Fahey was the inspired co-ordinator of the Southwark Irish Literary Society, a highly organised and successful Irish Studies and cultural activities body with a special youth programme built into its itinerary and which operated in South London in the 1890's. Ryan's experience and expertise deeply impressed Barclay, who mentioned him repeatedly, and indicated that he had read some of Ryan's output. Barclay described Ryan as "the most tolerant, broad-minded and scholarly of all the Irishmen I met in London."[22] Given Ryan's authoritative 1894 analysis of the Irish cultural revival in Britain – both in London and the rest of the country – Barclay may have felt stimulated to return to Leicester to foster similar developments.

Be that as it may, in 1902 on his return, he formed a branch of the Gaelic League at St Patrick's R.C. Elementary School in Royal East Street, near Abbey Street (which is still standing, and is sited next door to a local Irish club) and began to teach an Irish language class. This class, however, lasted less than a year. One reason for this was the still comparatively depressed status of the Irish in Leicester, socially and economically, at the end of the century. In 1872, Hugh Heinrick had described them thus: "with few exceptions they are literally the hewers of wood and the drawers of water",[23] a description which broadly matches the evidence available from census data analysis. This judgement is tentatively confirmed as still being partly the case in the 1890's – a quarter of a century later.[24]

The Irish language, then as now, was difficult to resource and sustain; Barclay was also actively represented in other important fields of Irish identity – traditional music, song and dance. The autobiography has frequent mentions of these facets of cultural activity, and Barclay emerges as a most positive influence and cultural reference point in two respects: as a well loved, popular and outward looking exponent of these arts, as well as being an informed and knowledgeable commentator on the history, traditions and folklore of the Irish. As an ambassador for Irish traditional culture, his work would still be sympathetically recognised by the Irish in Britain today. Barclay was no sentimentalist as regards Irish culture. He commented realistically: "I hope and trust that even if the old language dies out the old tunes will live. I know a good hundred and fifty of them, jigs, reels, planxties, suantrais, elegies and marches. In all the music I've heard what is there that can compare with them?"[25]

Evidence in the memoirs suggests that Barclay's musical appeal was strong not only inside but also outside the local Irish community. Formally and indeed informally, Barclay provides an early example of a tendency now recognised by today's commentators on aspects of identity amongst second generation Irish in Britain, America and elsewhere:-

> It comes as a surprise that the resurgence of interest in Irish identity places such little emphasis on Catholicism ... whereas the old identity was almost wholly Catholic-centred, the new one seeks its roots in Irish history, literature, music and art.[26]

Another aspect in which Barclay was ahead of his time as a pluralist interpreter of Irish identity was his willingness to accept and explore various differing aspects of Irish consciousness. In a discussion of Irish surnames and their derivations he remarked on the historical amalgam reflecting differing political and religious traditions and concluded: "all of which shows that we are a considerable mixture."[27]

Memoirs and Medleys has become a veritable quarry for historians of the Irish in Britain; inevitably, however, use has been selective, and, on occasions, ambiguous and misleading. The book has been much utilised by one local historian in studies of working-class life and urban popular culture, covering such topics as alcohol and tobacco use, and male occupation and leisure patterns.[28] Here, the emphasis has been on interpreting the Barclay family's similarities with other English working-class families; the Irish angle is indistinct and tangential. Writers of history at the national level have tended to do rather more justice to Barclay's Irish profile, but even here there has been imbalanced and questionable use made of the autobiography.

Although Barclay eventually became a prominent and widely respected secularist, much of his writing on Catholicism is explanatory and balanced. The awkward questions that he posed were not unfair intellectually; his writing reflected the style and content of nineteenth century Irish Catholicism as practised by Irish migrants in Britain. The description of his family's Catholic practice is profitably used as evidence by Raphael Samuel in a discussion of the Church and the Irish poor in a recent compilation about the Irish in the Victorian cities.[29] Similar use of Barclay's life is made by Lynn H. Lees in her key text about the Irish in Victorian London. As well as his mother's roles, already cited here, Samuel uses to good effect Barclay's account of his style of worship when a juvenile. In fact, Barclay offers much useful information on a range of religious matters: prayers, daily observances, ritual, superstition, religious manifestations in the home, the powerful emotional effects of a mission, and the constricting effects of Catholic Church-inspired intellectual censorship.[30] Although his beloved sister Kate had also become a freethinker, she returned to Catholicism not long before her death; Barclay, despite his own inclinations, happily paid for masses to be said for the repose of his sister's soul.[31]

Another topic Barclay is much-quoted on is the effects of anti-Irish prejudice and racism on the identity of the second generation Irish in Britain. Lees uses a key section of Barclay's reflections, where he is commenting on his mother's religiosity (quoted above). Lees prefaces this as follows: "... as a child Barclay turned away from both the language and the culture transmitted through it," and she then quotes from this passage:

But what had I to do with all that? I was becoming English! I did not hate things Irish, but I began to feel that they must be put away: they were inferior to things English. How could it be otherwise? My pronunciation was jeered at, - mimicked, corrected. I pronounced TEA "tay" like Alexander Pope used to do instead of pronouncing it "tee" as your present-day speaker does. Outside the house everything was English: my catechism, lessons, prayers, songs, tales, games – "English, quite English." Presently, I began to feel ashamed of the jeers and mockery and criticism, and tried to pronounce like the English. I had yet to learn that these same English were slangy, and ungrammatical, and continually mispronounced their own language. [32]

While Lees does acknowledge that Barclay's rejection was a child's transient response, and was an accurate reflection of some very real problems, she does not quote Barclay's reflective strictures on the use of English by the English themselves. More problematically, she gives no hint of Barclay's eventual commitment to key facets of Irish cultural identity, facets he was proud of and which were acknowledged by friends outside the Irish community.

Lees' incomplete representation is compounded in a more recent work by Graham Davis, on the Irish in nineteenth century Britain in which he cites Lees' reference to the *Memoirs*, and comments baldly: "How many young Irish people were like Tom Barclay ... and turned away from Irish language and culture?"[33] Davis would appear not to have had access to Barclay's text, and therefore does justice neither to Barclay as an individual in the sense of his re-awakening and long-term commitment, nor to those significant elements in the Irish community who were actively engaged in cultural transmission. The inability to be aware of this aspect is a recurring problem with research about the Irish in Britain, where researchers have academic skills but lack the cultural framework and contacts to research the sub-culture at its roots. The question which historians could more pertinently pose is: how many young Irish people, living in mainstream British society and culture, get a reasonable opportunity to sample and evaluate their cultural roots, and can do so in an atmosphere free from a deep-rooted anti-Irish prejudice in British society?

As well as some of the academics, others have left their own views of Barclay, and these are unanimous in that they are all positive. Although "grass-roots" research and oral history are difficult to evaluate, it has been established that Tom Barclay had made a wide local impact. This impact embraced the Irish community in the town. Barclay mentions a "Dom Macarthy" as a worthy friend; Macarthy was in many respects a reasonably "successful" Irish immigrant in terms of his high profile in local working-class politics. He became a leading figure in the Leicester Co-operative movement and in the Boot and Shoe Union; his two daughters were, despite being second generation Irish, enthusiastic learners, and then teachers, of Irish music, language and dance; and the family built up a respectable library of Irish interest texts, which covered poetry, drama, novels, music, song and dance, socialism and nationalism. The core of the collection is a representative cross-section of material from the Cultural Revival of the 1890's through to the nationalist and patriotic offerings of the 1916 period. Macarthy's son John (lately deceased) clearly recalled Barclay's visits to the family, and the cultural and political interaction which resulted. Of the children, this son, unlike the daughters, was basically untouched by his Irish cultural inheritance, although he did remain a staunch Catholic. So the Macarthy children exhibited the full spectrum of reaction by the second generation Irish to their cultural inheritance – a reaction which owed a great deal to the cultural skills and contacts provided by Tom Barclay.[34]

To summarise Barclay's achievement adequately is difficult: this is partly because his autobiography has been out of print for so many years. A reading of his life is almost an indispensable exercise for an observer who wishes to appreciate accurately the historical context of the pressures and experiences witnessed by the Irish in Britain today, whatever their generation. Much of what Barclay had to say about life in the three quarters of a century from c.1850 – 1935 is still relevant in terms of current issues affecting Anglo-Irish relations and the Irish in Britain. The availability of *Memoirs and Medleys* again, after sixty years, offers an opportunity to learn from the past, quite literally.

Of Tom Barclay personally, some brief quotations from obituaries complete the picture. His complex personality is summed up by Sydney Gimson, a leading local fellow secularist:

Many a good argie-bargie have I had with Tom and his cheery friendship has cheered me on my way. His intellectual gifts have always been greater than his practical common sense and he has had a hard life, always borne bravely and unselfishly.[35]

The notice in the *Leicester Mercury* concluded: "Always a man who was fond of an argument, and a fighting spirit at heart, Tom Barclay mellowed as he grew older, but his Irish disposition kept him a keen critic as well as an optimist." [36] The final reflection should perhaps rest with Gimson who knew Barclay well over a long period and who contributed the foreword to his autobiography. He remarked of Tom Barclay that:

He was wonderfully gifted in many ways ... I believe his life was a happy one though it makes one's blood boil to think of such a man living under such hard conditions. Friends would have been glad to make his last few years easier for him, but he was too independent to accept help so long as he could scrape along. It hurt sometimes to see him in his shabby old garments but he wore them with an unconscious dignity which carried a lesson for many of us.[37]

References.

1   BALDWIN, M., Tom Barclay – The Man Who Lived for Ideas; *Leicester Mercury* of 12 June 1963.

2   *Leicester Mercury*, obituary article; 2 January 1933, p.1.

3   The recurring tradition of celebrating the memory and ideas of local Protestant leaders is examined at length in the present author's doctoral research, Thesis on the Irish and Leicester, 1841-91, where full references are provided. This pattern can be traced to two levels: the local press, and local reports and pamphlets printed

throughout the last century by various Protestant (and often anti-Catholic) pressure groups.

4   Refer to files of *Leicester Journal* and *Leicester Mercury* in Leics. Record Office for further details. Leicester Record Office.

5   Various standard (but out-of-print) histories of the 17th Regiment of Foot can be consulted at the LRO.

6   For a full discussion of the varied reasons behind anti-Irish prejudice see O'TUATHAIGH, G., The Irish in Nineteenth - century Britain; Problems of Integration, in SWIFT, R. and GILLEY, S., *The Irish in the Victorian City*, Croom Helm (1985), pp. 13-36.

7   BARCLAY, T., *Memoirs and Medleys – the Autobiography of a Bottle Washer*, Leicester (1934) p.5.

8   *ibid*, p.5.

9   *ibid*, p.8.

10   *ibid*, pp. 6 and 7.

11   JACKSON, J. (Ed), *Open University Course* Unit E 354, Block 3, Part 3, The Irish in Britain, p.74; para 3-6.

12   DAVIS, G., *The Irish in Britain 1815-1914*, Gill & Macmillan (1991), Ch. 1; pp. 10-50

13   Barclay, T., *Memoirs*, p.11. He gave a much better and more analytical account of the reasons for migration, and of anti-Irish prejudice, in his account of Leicester slum districts in the *Wyvern* in the mid-1890's.

14   *ibid*, p.23

15   *ibid*, pp.10 and 11

16   *ibid*, p.6

17   BUTLER, R., *Life and Times of Bishop Ullathorne 1806-1889*, Vol. II (1926); pp.141-4

18   ELLIOT, B., (1987), 100th Anniversary booklet, Leicester police; and photo exhibition (now removed, 1993) in Guildhall Museum, where the issuing of cutlasses in 1867 was wrongly ascribed to the Chartist agitation, instead of the Fenian scares. There is a display of several of these weapons in the foyer of the new Leicestershire Police H.Q. at Enderby, near the M1 Junction.

19   Barclay, T., *Memoirs*, p.62

20   *Leicester Chronicle* and *Mercury*, 13 May 1882

21 Barclay, T., *Memoirs*, pp. 138-9

22 *ibid*, p.100

23 HEINRICK, H. (Ed. O'DAY, A.), *A Survey of the Irish in England* (1872/19)

24 This author's research database and 1891 Census evaluation. By 1891, Irish men had begun to enter more "blue collar" occupations, and some "white collar" jobs. A significant proportion of Irish women had become involved in Leicester's hosiery and knitwear trades.

25 Barclay, T., *Memoirs*, p.108. Interestingly, his informed and sympathetic views of his father's and mother's experiences was almost certainly reinforced by his readings of the progressive novels of the Banim brothers and the work of William Carleton on the Irish peasantry. It may also be the case that the balanced historical analysis found in the Banims' novels helped Barclay to develop his critical and balanced historical sensitivity.

26 SKERRETT, E., The Catholic Dimension; in McCAFFREY, L.J. et al., *The Irish in Chicago*, Univ. of Illinois Press, (1987); pp.43-44 and 47

27 Barclay, T., *Memoirs*, p.107

28 e.g. HAYNES, B., Aspects of Working Class Life in Leicester c.1845-80; in *Bulletin of Local History, E.Mids. Region*, Dept. of Ad. Ed., Univ. of Nottm., Vol.24/5, 1989-90, pp.5-24; HAYNES, B., Working Class Perception: Aspects of the Experience of Working Class Life in Victorian Leicester in *Trans. of Leics. Arch. and Hist. Soc.* LXIII, 1989, (Ed WILLIAMS, D.) pp.71-83

29 SAMUEL, R., The Roman Catholic Church and the Irish Poor; in SWIFT, R. and GILLEY, S. (1985) (Eds) *The Irish in the Victorian City*, Croom Helm, London p.283 and pp.286-7; LEES, L.H. (1979), *Exiles of Erin, Irish Migrants in Victorian London*, Cornell Univ. Press, N.Y., USA.

30 Barclay, T., *Memoirs*, pp. 26-30; 113-4; 116

31 *ibid*, p.122

32 LEES, see above, footnote 29

33 Davis, G. (1991), *The Irish in Britain, 1815-1914*, Gill Macmillan pp. 146-7

34 The information re the Macarthy family was gleaned from an oral history interview by the present author; the collection of books referred to includes works, some of them rare, by Markiewicz,

MacDonagh, Pearse, Connolly et al., which are now located in a reference collection in the Irish Studies Workshop in Leicester.

35 Gimson, G.A., *Random Recollections of the Leicester Secular Society* (typescript, 20 March 1932), Leicester Records Office.

36 *Leicester Mercury*, 2 January 1933, p.1.

37 Barclay, T., *Memoirs*, Foreword pp. x and xi.

CHAPTER I. CHILDHOOD

WAS I dreaming, or was I awake, or was I between the two ? What does it matter ? What *does* matter is that this my first consciousness, my first recollection, is one of intense fear. I was a little child alone in the upper room of a hovel. It was night and all was silent—not a soul near. I may have been sleeping, I do not know ; but by the dim light of a tallow candle I saw a harrowing vision, or phantom—what should I call it—a black thing shaped like a bird, in size somewhat between a sparrow and a crow and crested like a peacock, that fluttered round the candle and poised over me between the bed and the ceiling. I felt that it hated me with a malignant hatred. Did I cry out, or was I mute, paralysed with terror ? Perhaps I swooned ; perhaps I was convulsed. I think my mother, dear loving mother, must have come and clasped me, and soothed me, or I might have died, but I remember nothing of what occurred immediately before or after the cursed vision.

What do you mean, old Petronius, by saying *"Primus in orbe Deus fecit timor"* ? Why did I fear ? Why was it not some other emotion ? Are timidity and cowardice, I wonder, engendered by such frights as this ? I am wondering too, seventy years now after, why the phantom was in the shape of a bird, of all creatures the blithe happy being most like what we conceive of angels. And talking of angels where was *my* guardian angel during my terror ?

Has he affairs of his own, saying "Why should I be
my mortal brother's keeper?" I have since thought
that one's guardian angel cannot guard, but only
regret after his charge has been sinning or suffering.
The good God too, I must assume that He sat serenely
in His heaven, looking on seemingly without feeling
—but what was such a little matter compared with
shipwrecks, plagues, earthquakes, wars and catas-
trophies in general? A mere nothing; but it was
much to the poor little child, me. I wish He was less
concerned with the fall of sparrows, and the number
of hairs on a person's head, and would really pity us
His special creatures, "like as a father pitieth his
children." Perhaps there were tens of thousands of
innocent little child-wretches on this same night
suffering similarly in hovels and the equivalent of
hovels up and down the world. But hadn't they also
joys and pleasures, it may be asked? I hope so, but
why not be joyous all the time, like the angels?
Perhaps there were little joys in *my* childhood, but if
there were they never impressed me; I do not remember them as I do this hellish nightmare. Perhaps
joys are superficial—surface things that float and fade
from memory, while griefs and torments cut deep.

I spoke just now of God "*sitting*," and I called my
guardian angel "*he*"; if you notice there are no women-
angels; Michael, Gabriel, Raphael, Ithuriel, are all
gentlemen : what physical words and images are we
not driven to in attempting to deal with the spiritual !

My next remembrance is one of disappointment,
unsatisfied desire. How low must that state of poverty
be in a family where the child, and he the only child,

has to scratch a brick of the floor with a splinter of slate for want of a pencil. I had toddled into the street and saw a fragment of slate-pencil—a strayed two-inch fragment—below the threshold of a door-way ; I knew instinctively that it would write and draw smoothly. I desired it with a great desire, but— alas ! I dared not reach for it. I hesitated, and while hesitating another little one put forth his hand, and it was his. What a monotonous childhood ! No toys, no picture-books, no pets, no going "ta-ta." No carpet on the uneven brick floor, no mat, no wall-paper ; what poverty ! There was neither doctor nor midwife present at my birth ; of that I am convinced. Indeed I have heard mother boast that she never needed a midwife. She was very hardy, brought up in the wilds of the "county Mayo, God help us ! " After all, why shouldn't a woman be able to bring forth like cats and cows and other mammals ?

Here in this eighteen foot square court off Burley's Lane, Leicester, St. Margaret's bells rang dismally every Sunday morning as I tried to play with duck-stones for toys. I'm afraid the one door and one chamber window of the two-roomed crib we lived in were seldom opened, though not six feet from the muck hole and the unflushed privies, and air could only get in from one side of the house. How did we remain healthy ? But let me not imagine that because others were born in country cottages and manses with meads that slope away in front and wind swept hills in view that therefore they lived happy ever after. Open-air exercises, a sumptuous table, purple and fine linen and a University education awaiting,

yes : but in spite of all these, they will suffer dis-
appointments, boredom, weariness—perhaps poverty
—and some will murder or be murdered, while poverty-
stricken *moi qui parle* may end up calm as a Buddha
and in tune with the Infinite.

After the monotony and dreariness of that Burley's
Lane hut, I somehow find myself in a similar two-
roomed hut in a similar court in a similar slum—
Abbey Street : our walls are now plastered with wood-
cuts from newspapers, and there are mounds of
thick ice all round the gutters. Now there are five of
us sleeping in one little upper room. I remember
nothing of this locale but the attitudinising of kiddies
in the yard doubling their fists and prattling of the
great fight between Sayers and Heenan. We were
commanded to remain shut in, father and mother
being out most of the day earning a living. Father
knew no trade and to dig was not able : he collected
rags and bones, rag-bag on back, without as much as
a truck (or handcart) : mother worked at a rag-shop
or marine store dealer's, or she got blocks of wood
from the woodyards, chopped them small and sold
the chips in pen'norths for fire-lighting round the
neighbouring streets.

"Now see that ye don't stir a foot out of this
till me or yer mother comes back, or I'll tan the
life out of ye, do ye hear ? "
Such the command, but it wasn't in juvenile flesh and
blood to obey always.

The scene changes once more, and we are again
still in a two-roomed pigsty-crib in a court off Woodboy Street, but all dreariness is gone, exchanged for

alarms and excursions, chases and flights and mad uproar. How could anyone resist breaking out of that dirty kennel on a summer's day when the sun shone even into that court. We broke bounds and ran up and down the street like little mad things. Why had we to stay in? Well, you see, we might get lost or run over or beaten—hounded and ill used by the Sassenach kids : as a matter of fact we were hounded and harrassed.

"Hurroo Mick ! "

"Ye Awrish Paddywack."

"Arrah, bad luck to the ships that brought ye over ! "

These were the salutes from the happy English child : we were battered, threatened, elbowed, pressed back to the door of our kennel amid boos and jeers and showers of small missiles. The unkind expressions must have been borrowed from the grown-ups whose animosity was often evident enough. To tell the truth, Sassenach kids fought among themselves ; street fought street and district district without the slightest cause. And after all, why expect youths (who are mentally but at the stone-age period) not to fight without cause while grown-ups, backed and abetted by college professors and ministers of Jesus Christ, fight with almost as little ? I would like to know, and I wish I were anthropologist and psychologist enough to answer, is there any such reality as race-hatred ? There should not be among intelligent grown-up people. My own attitude towards a foreigner of whatever colour or creed is simply one of interest— intense curiosity. And this makes me social : the only thing that might repel me, or make me cold, is denseness, want of mentality ; but this repels me in men of my own nationality. India, Aryan mother of many gods and heroes and sages and of several civilizations, as I have read, Hail ! Hail China and Japan and Burmah ! Read Edward Carpenter and Fielding Hall on these lands. Read Maspero on Ancient Egypt. Teuton and Frank, Saxon and Celt, Ulsterman and Munsterman, read and don't be fools. Dear humane brilliant thinker and writer John Ruskin, whom few I'm afraid now read, what a sensible and noble way you had of regarding it. The Irishman differs from the Scot, the Cambrian from the Tyneside man : let each emulate the other : let us copy the characteristics that are best in one another. Surely, being on different sides of the River Rhine was no real *Casus Belli* in 1870 : you had no more reason for fighting—you, French and Germans —than we kids of Woodboy Street had for fighting the kids of Foundry Lane. Religion seems as powerless with this superstition of Boundary as it is with the vagaries of Fashion.

Fenianism is rife about this time : I remember our parents rejoicing over the escape from prison of— the Head Centre, James Stephens (I think it was) :— Also, we were greatly excited by the news of the blowing up of Clerkenwell Prison. We lamented the hanging of the Manchester Martyrs, and our English neighbours danced and rejoiced. What wonder ? Some priest said hell was not hot enough for the Fenians.

Whenever an English man or woman did anything disreputable, my mother was wont to remark "Ah

well, sure, what better could one expect from the
breed of King Harry ? " The Sassenach was regarded
by us with a mixture of contempt and hatred. God
had made him it is true and Jesus Christ had died to
save him, but we clean forgot that, and only saw
him embodied in Calvin and Cranmer, the lustful
King Henry VIII, Queen Bess the Persecutor, the
Orangeman's idol, William of Orange, and "the
bloody Cromwell." There were though a few good
Englishmen no doubt, like Alfred the Great, Sir
Thomas Moore, and William Cobbett who wrote the
history of the Protestant Reformation. My father
was a Limerick man, and we were often hearing
eulogies of the hero Patrick Sarsfield, and the women
of Limerick who fought and repelled the English
during the siege of that city. How we gloated over the
way the Irish Brigade defeated the English at Fonte-
noy ! But what filthy little wretches we children were,
and how could it be otherwise ? Not Papuans nor
Basutos nor Fijians could I think be more degraded.
And this was in the middle of the nineteenth century.
O great and glorious empire ! What chance to be
clean was there in a house on whose only floor bags
of dusty rags and putrescent bones were spilled out
to be sorted ? Nevertheless, we were used to this, and
before going to bed we all knelt down, after a supper
of Indian meal, on the bare uneven brick floor and
recited the Rosary, father leading off : one Our Father
to ten Hail Mary's : one of the prayers spoken fifty
times by the help of a string of beads : and we arose
feeling good and comforted and strengthened for the
morrow's work.

I don't know what a Buddhist Praying Wheel is like, but here's a sketch of the Rosary-beads : the three nearest the Cross represent the Trinity : the large ones are for the "Our Father."

We used to say very devoutly "Forgive us our trespasses as we forgive them that trespass against us," and we used to forget that we very seldom did forgive.

One day the kids from the other end of the court, or "yard," as we called it, attacked us under Billy, their leader, and broke a pane of glass and thrust a rod through : unable to get out, or fearful of a spanking if we did, we scuttled upstairs and threw cinders from the chamber window on Billy and his pals : they battered the door, and we retaliated as we could. My imagination went to work : Billy was King William and we were the Irish : it was the siege of Limerick being in some mysterious manner enacted over again. There it was Gael and Sassenach once more. What neighbours quarrels when father and mother came back, what fine excuses for our conduct, why shouldn't we defend ourselves ? There followed weltings and wailings, but I can't blame father and mother for venting their anger : the whole crib from floor to roof showed but too horribly a state of siege.

What sort of an existence was it where a mother

giving suck had to be hours away from home trying to earn something ? When the kids of the yard were not molesting us, I as eldest was nurse, and often have I put my tongue into baby's mouth to be sucked in lieu of "titty" to stop her cries. The cries used to cease for a minute, and then were resumed as the tongue gave no satisfaction. Poor cooped-up vermin-infested brats ! But I am suffering much more now probably in simply remembering our state than I actually suffered then : we did not feel the dimness and squalor and foul smells—the horror of the bugs and lice and black-beetles—as I now, many years after feel them : we had no other life, no other sensations and feelings. This was life, and we knew no other to contrast it with. Does the worm wish to be a butterfly, or the mole a lark ?

What is "chin-cough" and how should it be cured ? I suspect chin-cough was whooping-cough : mother's cure for it was a drink out of the chalice. I and my brother were taken to the chapel, and kneeling before the altar-rails, the kind priest gave us a drink out of the sacramental chalice : I don't know was the liquor wine or water, or whether it cured us.

There is a proverb that the grey mare is often the best horse : mother was the grey mare of our family : untiring energy, unfailing health and hope and faith, and never a new dress, never a holiday, never any leisure or amusement, never I fear even a generous meal of victuals. All work and no play, but still not dull. I'm sure we never had a complete bath in all our childhood's years, unless such a thing is indispensable to the newly-born. Mother did all

that was possible, but she had neither time nor means
to boil our rags of shirts and sheets when washing.
We had no wash-tub nor dolly-pegs, not to speak of
wringing and mangling machines : there could have
been no room for such in a room only nine feet by
nine, even had we possessed them, eh, Mother ?
So we went unwashed, and pediculus thrived greatly
in his two principal species, *capitis* and *vestimenti*, and
God's beautiful image was preyed upon daily and
nightly. No fault of Mother's.

She was not permitted, even had she the money
and leisure, to indulge in beer and dominoes of an
evening like my father ; her consolation was an old
Irish lamentation or love song and the contemplation
of the sufferings of "Our Blessed Lord" and his
virgin mother. We males can revert to paganism
and forget for an hour or two in revel and song the
Man of Sorrows—the poor gibbetted God : where
now, while we are carousing, are Gethsemane and
Calvary ? We are lapped in the Elysium of ale and
skittles and cards. We are no Christians to-night,
we, but Bacchanals. The woman—the mother is at
the same time and hour kneeling at the feet of the
Blessed Virgin, or scheming and troubling how she
shall pay next week's shop and rent. We get credit
till Saturday from the little grocer's shop at the
corner, but we must pay each Saturday or have to
go hungry all next week.

I don't know why father felt entitled to think
Munster superior to Connaught unless it was because
Limerick had had a siege, while Mayo was without
one. He had read Byron and Burns and Tom Moore,

but I often wonder how he acquired some twenty numbers of a periodical called *The Celt* ; he always pronounced the name "Selt" ; it was a Young Irelander periodical I believe, and if I'm spared to visit Ireland again I must make enquiries about it, for I have never seen or heard about it anywhere, or from anyone else. Poor father, what else could you do but drink, when you had the chance, which was not often, I think ? You and mother and the rest of the wretched emigrants, victims of the 1848 potato blight, I often think of your condition—the sad exodus—penniless—trade-less—never to return to Erin ! Did the famine-ships bring you over free ? Brother was separated from brother—whole families broken up : one remained in Liverpool, one in the Potteries, and one went to America. Women as well as men tramped every foot of the road after leaving the boats : no trains for mere emigrants. Stick selling, mat-making, rag and bone dealing and farm-labouring ; no possibility of learning a handicraft, and no hope of ever returning to your own country, "Exiles without defence and without shelter, lamenting their fatherland and their inheritance."

As with the previous dens, our door in the court in Woodboy Street was seldom open in summer and hardly ever in winter : it would never do to let the cold in. I suppose such exist even to this day. Two little rooms, one up and one down, and air, the air of a court too, having entrance and exit by one side of the house only. I say "to this day," and this is the year of 1924, of Wembley wonders and Empire pageants. Poor as we were we were not the poorest

in the court ; the very poorest were too proud to let
the others know how poor they were : they felt
shame of what they couldn't possibly help, as when
they broke the only saucepan in the house, and had
to borrow one.

Public houses were allowed to open far into the
night, and all night, at this period, and children of
any age were allowed to go in and out of them :
often have I gone to the Woodboy public house for a
farthing's worth of small beer.

We all had smallpox, and one of us died, and
then father began to drink more : and as if dirt and
dinginess and bickerings and hidings and rags and
assaults of vermin were not hell enough, we are
afeared of the Devil, that "Enemy of Mankind"
invisible but always at our elbow whispering in our
ear. See *Hell Open to Christians*, by Father Furniss
(or Furnace). I wonder whether Catholics have now
withdrawn it from circulation. When this frightened
us, we knelt down and recited The Rosary and
invoked our patron saints and guardian angels. Even
bandits and murderers and night-walkers have
guardian angels, I suppose. We were greatly comforted too by *The Glories of Mary*, written by St.
Alphonsus Liguori, a canonized Saint of the Church :
the Saint relates in that book that the Blessed Virgin
has actually brought back the damned from hell. I
remember an account in the same book of a brigand
who was being led to execution : on his way he had to
pass a statue of the Blessed Virgin. He was very
devout to the Mother of God, and asked permission
to kneel and pray before the statue : his request was

granted, and rising from his knees, about to set out again with his captors, the statue put out an arm and grasped *his* arm and detained him.   His captors couldn't possibly desecrate a statue of Mary, and if I remember aright, the criminal was pardoned, in deference to and reverence for the miracle.

CHAPTER II.—ADOLESCENCE

AND now I went to work : this would be about the year 1860. I was eight years of age and I went to work, turning the wheel at Browett's Rope-walk where Taylor Street now stands. Unwashed, ill-clothed, ill-fed, untaught, worried by vermin, I worked in all weathers, and not without scolding and threats of violence, seventy hours a week for—how much ? One shilling and sixpence. About a farthing an hour, think of it. There was no clock in the house, and many a morning have I dressed hurriedly at about five a.m. and run out into the street enquiring the time lest I should be late for six a.m. Oh what a happy land was England ! Later still I wound yarn for cardigan jacket weavers in Curzon Street, and I forget what time I started in the morning, but I know I worked until ten o'clock at night. At that time there was no legal restriction as to what age a child might go to work, nor to the number of hours a day you worked him. I remember I turned the wheel a spell at Colton's Rope-walk which was situated on the very ground now occupied by Cooper and Corah's place—St. Margaret's Works. When father came home boozed, there was a row in the house ; singing and shouting and abuse : we were all frightened and upset, and I used to be late at work through having my sleep curtailed, and so got the sack. Consequently I worked at a number of places. I was a boot-finisher's sweater, and peeled osier-rods on a plantation close by St. Mary's Mount in the Newarke : here I fell into the canal (or the Soar, I forget which) and was rescued from drowning. Finally I managed to learn something of the Hosiery Trade through being a Rotary Hand's helper. In the old bad Rope-walk days my diet consisted, on week-days, mainly of bread and treacle, but now I had a few coppers for myself : I used to buy ha'porth's of peas, or toss the penny pie-man in the street. You put down a penny on the lid of his can under cover of your hand, "Head or tail ? " you said : if he cried "head" and it was a head, you got nothing : on the other hand if he cried wrongly, you picked up your penny and got a pie for nothing.

The Glories of Mary, referred to earlier, and *Lives of the Saints* were borrowed from Holy Cross Lending Library on payment of a penny. There was no Free Library in those days ; I don't know who instituted it, but may his tribe increase ! I was one of the earliest borrowers : I could hardly believe the tidings of great joy. What, be able to get books without buying or renting ? I washed and titivated and sewed the rent in my trousers, and presented myself respectfully, diffidently. Yes, it was no fiction. What rapture ! *Handy Andy, Traits and Stories of the Irish Peasantry, Ivanhoe, Pickwick Papers, Adam Bede, The Last of the Mohicans.* I had read some Shakespeare before the Library opened. Dick's shilling edition in paper covers was owned by another Irish chap, one Jem Dillon, next door, a little better off than myself ; he lent it me as a great favour, but I could never get far until he wanted it back again : now I could borrow Shakespeare for a whole fortnight, aye, and then renew it. But Dick the publisher deserves a word of praise ; he did many a youth a grand service no doubt in bringing out that cheap edition of Shakespeare. Many a studious youth too, I take it, has blessed another publisher, namely Cassell, for bringing out the Popular Educator.

Why are youngsters unruly and disobedient ? I'll tell you. It's because we are a society in ourselves —a different species. We find that parents and elders are antiquated, behind the times, not to be trusted. They are envious. They have eaten of the forbidden fruit and their eyes are open, but why can't they let us too eat and have our eyes open ? So much that we like too they dislike. We like movement, they like rest : we love noise, they prefer quiet and silence. They are our enemies, continually interfering, restraining, repressing. Schoolmasters, priests, police, parents, are all in a conspiracy to withhold us from the joys of life. We are thought to be mischievous,— nonsense ! We are only playful, vitally ebullient, destructive by accident : isn't it natural for youth to be venturesome and to seek adventure ? How are heroes made ? Ask the author of *Alone in the Pirates' Lair* and *Deadwood Dick*. Here, boys, let us only stand together, then, "Come the whole world in arms and we shall shock them." We're the intrepid heroes and I'm leader : police are molesting trespassers : we're invincible. Authority ? Pooh, spell it tyranny. These elders are down on us : they don't want us to smoke and drink, yet they smoke and drink themselves. What's good for them is good for us, besides it's manly. Drink—ah, a grand thing !

Everyone talks of it at work, looks for it, goes to it.
Gin, rum, brandy, whisky, see how they glisten in the
bottles in the windows ; listen outside to how merry
they make the drinkers. So we went to the "Free
and Easy," and heard " Old Mother Gum " sung,
and "After the Opera's Over" and "Not for Joe"
and "It's Naughty but it's Nice." What is a "Free
and Easy" ? Simply a concert in a public house :
there were a round dozen of them in Leicester here
some forty years ago. I went and heard and drank.
How I made it consistent with going regularly to
Mass and attending the Rosary and Confession and
Holy Communion, monthly, is a mystery : but then,
isn't it a mystery that I believed in the commandment
"Thou shalt not kill," while greatly desiring to be a
pirate chief who runs up the Black Flag decorated
with the skull and crossbones, and makes his victims
walk the plank ? Inconsistency encore inconsistency.
tonjours inconsistency.

Listen to some of the hymns we used to sing.
Here's a verse alluding to the devils in hell :—

> "The cursed crew have lost their treasure,
> That endless joy that knows no measure,
> And now with reckless envy burning
> Their fury on our souls are turning."

Do you think so my dear hymnologist ? It seems to
me that souls in torment would be unable to feel
envy, or anything else but the torment. If they are
being tormented all the time (or all the eternity)
they can have very little energy to expend except in
suffering. But perhaps I'm making a mistake and that
the author of this hymn means the devils that go

about like roaring lions, seeking whom they may
tempt on earth : perhaps God mitigates or remits
their tortures so that they can successfully carry on
business and inveigle souls to Hell.   The hymn
goes on

> "Arm for deadly fight,
> Earth and Hell unite
> And swear in lasting bonds to bind us
> *   *   *   *   *
> With Jesus still the foe shall find us."

Earth unites with hell it seems ; but earth is we,
ourselves.   How and when does it (or do we) swear
to unite ?   Our own kind, our own brothers are
called our "foes."   Hellish or earthly, we are creatures
of this same Jesus who said, "Love your enemies."
Look at the consistency here and the sweet charity !
Another hymn was

> "We must march to the battle with speed,
> Upon earth our one duty is strife ;
> How blest are the soldiers who bleed
> For the Saviour who died to give Life."

Many a time and oft have we read and been told that
Jesus bled for man, but that man should bleed for
Jesus is to say the least a strange new doctrine.   Yet
another hymn addresses St. Catherine of Sienna
re the Pope.—

> "Holy Mother, guard our pontiff,
> Raging billows round him foam ;
> Saint seraphic, still the tempest,
> Aid the Church and pray for Rome."

This invocation seems to doubt the very words of
Jesus Christ Himself.   Did He not, through Peter, give

the keys of the Kingdom of Heaven to the Pope,
and did He not say the Gates of Hell should not
prevail against His Bride the Church ?

I used to sing these hymns, rapt, overflowing with
emotion.   Not only so, but Protestant hymns disgusted me, and I actually used to spit out to cleanse
my mouth if I thoughtlessly had been singing a
strain caught from some pious shop-mates, such as

"There is a fountain filled with blood."

Bigotry you may say (I'm assuming here that I shall
have readers) Bigotry. Well, I'm not sure that earnest-
ness in belief does not carry with it a certain amount
of bigotry. You see, you know you've got the very
truth of God, and how can you then be tolerant of and
lenient to falsehood and error ? Away with them !
Stamp them out, they are wicked ! I'm sure the
Inquisitors and Crusaders, and persecutors have felt
that they were doing a great service to Almighty
God in doing as they did. But what banality these
hymns I have quoted. Let no cultured Catholic
pretend they are superior to the crudest vapourings
of the Salvation Army.

I entirely ignored the value of fresh air in these
days ; cribbed and cabined either at home, or at
chapel, or in the factory : for ever in some building.
Poor fool ! At the end of the day's work you have
opportunity to go into the fresh air, walk out into
the fields, but no. An old clothes-basket of books is
pulled over towards the chamber window—second-
hand, often tattered books, picked up from stalls in
the market : discarded school-books with copious

notes telling of "filthy loves of gods and goddesses."
Ovid, Juvenal, Catullus—just for the notes in English,
for we have no Latin outside the ordinary of the Mass.
What information, how strange, how intensely
interesting. Jupiter, Juno, Mars, Apollo, Neptune,
Vulcan, Pluto, Mercury, Venus, Minerva, Pan,
Nymphs, Fauns, Satyrs, Dryads, Fates, Furies, Muses,
Harpies. There we sat rapt, exchanging our health
for what ?—Listen. So and so (I forget his name)
"whose fifty daughters Hercules deflowered (or
debauched) in one night." There's stuff for big or
little Christians to imbibe ! I don't know though
was it any worse than the fiction-stuff I read at this
period : it came out in penny weekly numbers, and
the titles are about enough to show of what it consisted. Among others, I read with keen relish *Houns-
low Heath and its Moonlight Riders, Starlight Bess,
Queen of the Highwaymen, Black Rollo the Pirate
Chieftain, or the Dark Woman of the Deep, The Skeleton
Horseman or the Shadow of Death, Admiral Tom, Boy
King of the Buccaneers* and *Spring-heeled Jack the
Terror of London.* Soon, all too soon, I got to the end
of a number and read "To be continued in our next."
How exciting it was when Admiral Tom, at bay,
snatches up a lighted torch, or takes a pistol from his
belt (I forget now which), and setting a foot on the
something or other of the powder magazine, threatens
to blow the ship, himself, crew and all, sky-high.
Spring-heeled Jack too : how unaccountably they have
left him out of the annals of crime and adventure.
Somewhere about the sixties all London was at his
mercy.   Those astounding springs on his boots

enabled him to soar over the house-tops like a rocket
and do whatever he darned pleased. He was never
shot down nor captured nor injured ; he could always
escape. It never occurred to the youthful mind to
enquire on what principle of mechanics boot and
springs could be contrived that would project a man
lightly and rapidly over house-tops. But the hero has
to be perfect ; he can do no wrong more than a god,
and he never makes a mistake. If he gets captured
it is only to show how easily he can escape and wreak
vengeance on his enemies. Ha, ha ! When you die
at his peerless dauntless hands there is no murder
committed : when his dagger enters your heart you
feel that it is a meritorious and glorious consumma-
tion to perish thus. Father, aye, even mother, in
odd moments of leisure scanned my weekly penny
number and became infected with admiration of
Black Rollo's deeds of derring-do. Never check or
thwart the hero, O writers of the so-called Penny
Dreadful ; but of course you will not ; your readers
would desert you an you did, their world would
crumble. Go on depicting him tall, graceful, majestic,
handsome ; sinews like a Hercules, and features like
a Hyperion : and you illustrators, show him fierce
and scowling with leg advanced, ready to spring to
the attack that means the certain defeat of his foes :
for my part I feel greatly obliged to you for producing
such admirable super-men as Black Rollo the Pirate,
and Spring-heeled Jack. After all, are the productions
of your Rider Haggard's and your Marie Corelli's,
that are absorbed by grown-ups of to-day, much more
natural or probable than the Black Rollo and Sweeney

Todd and Spring-heeled Jack of immature young
minds ? Similarly in the realm of song. Sixty years
ago you had "Old Bob Ridly" and "Champagne
Charley" and "Tommy Make Room for Your Uncle"
in everybody's mouth : "Burgundy Benjamin" and
"Champagne Charley" were hymned by tens of
thousands who probably never tasted a drop of
Burgundy or Champagne in all their lives : the tippler
as hero, nothing less. But let none dare say we have
improved on that in sixty years, seeing that now we
gleefully chuntle "Where do Flies go in the Winter-
time" ? and manufacture a song out of the triviality
that a fruiterer has sold out all of his bananas. Have
we progressed in song ? Turn to the sweet old folk-
songs, English, Irish, Scottish, Welsh, and see and
hear for yourself. More of this anon : meanwhile,
how is it that when a really good modern song
arrives we soon let it die. "Alice where art thou ? "
Where indeed ? And "Queen of the Earth" you
deserved a much longer reign ; your words are real
poetry. Have you ever heard "When first I met you
on the Village Green?"—a really charming thing, both
words and music. By-the-by, I'm not sure of the
title ; it may be called (probably is) "Sweet Sixteen."

I never went to day-school, only to Sunday-school,
and for a while to night-school ; but night-school
was mixed—boys and girls, and we were far more
interested in one another than in learning : we were
beginning to rehearse the drama of sex. Dear old
school-master John Mee, you were a gentleman, and
if I mistake not, a real saint. How was my propensity
to draw and sketch brought over from some previous

generation, I wonder. I never saw father draw nor
sketch, and mother never could write her own name.
My brick scratching with slate splinters in infancy
must have remained unnoticed, I think.   Mother
taught me to spell and read.   She was held to be
quite exceptional among her countrywomen in that
she could read Dr. Gallacher's sermons in Irish. This
Gallacher was the bishop of Raphoe in Donegal.
How she who read English with difficulty could read
these sermons, though in Roman characters, with
their transliteration nearly as bad as Welsh, is something I do not understand : but read them she could,
and often have I seen the tears come into her eyes
over the sermon on the passion of Our Lord.   This
she used to read on a Good Friday. "Glory to God
but you're the one ! " neighbours used to exclaim.
It did them good to hear a blessed sermon read in the
first language they ever spoke. I don't know was her
maiden name MacLin or Maglyn, for I never saw it
written ; her mother's people were O'Reillys.   She
was well acquainted with the old legends of Oisin,
and Fin, and Cuchullan, and the Gobawn Sayr, and
could sing and recite a goodly number of old Irish
songs and poems. The old bardic legends and laments
and love songs must have been transmitted orally
from generation to generation for centuries : they
were crooned and told round the turf fire of a winter's
night.   But what had I to do with all that ? I was
becoming English ! I did not hate things Irish, but I
began to feel that they must be put away ; they were
inferior to things English. How could it be otherwise ?
My pronunciation   was   jeered   at,—mimicked,

corrected. I pronounced TEA "tay" like Alexander
Pope used to do instead of pronouncing it "tee" as
your present-day speaker does. Outside the house
everything was English : my catechism, lessons,
prayers, songs, tales, games—"English, quite English."
Presently, I began to feel ashamed of the jeers and
mockery and criticism, and tried to pronounce like
the English. I had yet to learn that these same English
were slangy, and ungrammatical, and continually
mispronounced their own language. Poverty was
accepted by mother with the patience of Job. "Why
shouldn't we suffer when Our Blessed Lord Himself
suffered ? Didn't He say blessed are the poor, and
didn't His divine lips tell us to lay up treasure in
Heaven ? Sure none of us—not even the Saints—
will ever fast forty days, or suffer a bloody sweat.
Glory be to His Divine Name to think that we have
the Light of Faith, and that His Blessed Mother and
the Saints are praying and interceding for us ! What
matters what we may suffer in this miserable life, and
isn't it for our sins ? "

About this time I must have been a strange mixture,
or everything by starts and nothing long. I want to
be a painter and with the painters stand. I study a
book of replicas of engravings by Michael Angelo ;
I paint the Blessed Virgin in water-colours, positive,
red, blue, and yellow ; roses in cheeks, halo, and
smile, and perfectly regular young features, too
modest to look at one, just as I had seen her on
foolish religious cards, in fact, idealised out of all
semblance to reality. That's on Monday. I want
to be an actor—a tragedian, one that shall eclipse

Keane and Macready and leave Barry Sullivan far
behind. That's Tuesday. On Wednesday I would
like to be a monk. Thursday I study Latin, and want
to know from the priest how I can obtain the *Summa
Theologica* of St. Thomas Aquinas. There have been
in the Church a subtle doctor, a profound doctor,
a seraphic doctor : I don't know what I may be,
but, oh to be learned ! No, I'll be an artist or a
musician ; this is Friday. On Saturday my shop-
mates challenge me to go and have a drink or two at
a "Free and Easy," and I go, and now I mean to be a
comedian, a singer, an entertainer. Drink, ah, a great
thing, a manly thing ! No danger ; everybody drinks,
and talks about drink, and looks for drink, and
boasts about drink.

Let not poverty-stricken parents think that children
are going to help them as soon as they (the children)
earn a few coppers : two things would be necessary
for that—*means* and *thought*. Was he criminal ? He
had earned a few coppers, but he never thought about
father or mother or little sisters : he didn't think at
all. His catechism told him that he came to the use
of reason at seven years, or thereabout ; well, he
was now eleven years, but if he had reason he never
used it. Shall we call him a young scamp ? He has
ended his week's work. He was like a prisoner escaped
from his cell, a bird released from the cage : he has
left the loathsome den of a place called home for an
hour or two and craves to see "The Vampire's
Bride" at the theatre. He is clad in second-hand
duds, his boots are bad, and his stockings are holed,
yet almost the first coppers he handles are not hoarded

nor laid out wisely and well, but go for the excitement
of seeing "The Vampire's Bride." Cost you three-
pence, it did. True he had never seen a pantomime
at Christmas, had never been a journey by rail, had
never had a day in the country, had never been in the
woods, had had no amusement or recreation of any
kind but a school tea-party, or an hour by some
pond, stutting ; stickleback catching that is. What
ought we to have expected of him ? I wonder if any
ancestor of his for twenty generations ever had money
enough to make a world tour, or even a Continental
tour. Were we always poor ? Have we been the
thralls of Chieftains from the time of the first settlers
in Ireland ? I suppose I shall never see Naples, the
Egæan, Paris, Devon, Cornwall, Princes Street,
Edinburgh, the Giants' Causeway, Snowden, Killarney,
Ione, Peele, Rome, Madrid, Venice, the Rhine. But
I trust that some day a visit to some three or four of
these places will be a possibility in the lives of all, of
whatever rank, who desire it.

Just now I am very religious. Every morning on
awakening and dressing I make the sign of the Cross
from forehead to breast and from shoulder to shoulder,
uttering "In the name of the Father, and of the Son,
and of the Holy Ghost, Amen." I say the Our
Father, Hail Mary, and Apostle's Creed, and invoke
the Holy Family—

"Jesus, Mary, Joseph, I offer my heart and life.
Jesus, Mary, Joseph, assist me in my last agony.
Jesus, Mary, Joseph, may I die in peace in your blessed
    company."

Every day of the week is devoted by the pious Catholic

to some saint or pious conception ; thus—Monday
to the Holy Ghost ; Tuesday, the Holy Angels ;
Wednesday, St. Joseph ; Thursday, the Blessed
Sacrament ; Friday, the Crucifixion ; Saturday, the
Blessed Virgin ; and Sunday, of course, to the Blessed
Trinity. There are, I learn, nine choirs of Angels :
I do not now remember them all, but I remember
there are Thrones, Powers, Principalities, Dominions,
Cherubs, Seraphs, Archangels and ordinary angels :
I don't know who's responsible for the category. The
other denizens of Heaven are also categorized, as for
instance Martyrs, Confessors, Innocents, Patriarchs.
The months are devoted like the days. May is the
month of Mary, June the month of Jesus, November
is devoted to the Holy Souls in Purgatory, and
December to the Nativity of Our Lord.

I would never at this time of which I write have
dared to set foot in Protestant Church or Dissenting
Chapel ; I don't know what commandment I would
have been breaking, but I know it was taboo. The
places were unclean, abhorrent. As soon think of
entering a temple of Ashtaroth : and don't talk to
me about us all worshipping the same God : in this
wide realm of Religious Sectarianism we are governed
by feeling, not thought. Every non-catholic is a
Heretic or a Pagan. Oh yes, I was very devout :
something like what the Irish call a voteen. I chalked
an altar on the bare brown wall of the chamber
where six of us slept, father, mother, and four children:
I sketched candles, three each side of a tabernacle,
and a crucifix above it in the centre, all in chalk.
Oh how I wished to be a great painter. Michael

Angelo, Rafael, Correggio, Tintoretto, Titian, Da
Vinci, Cimabue, Rubens, Rembrandt, Velasquez,
Veronese,—I knew their names towards it, anyway ;
the only other things wanted were hard study of
such things as light, shade, perspective, foreshortening,
chiaroscuro,—money for tuition and leisure, a
studio, perseverance, and—genius.

And now came along the "Mission": non-Catholics
will understand if I say that a Mission is a "Revival."
I am not going to say that it is a special message from
the Almighty, but it has been instituted by His
priests ; therefore take heed.   Strange !   The Ten
Commandments had been kept as well as those of the
Church.   Holy Mass was celebrated every morning
and was attended every Sunday under pain of Mortal
Sin, and everyone knows Mortal Sin kills the soul
and deserves Hell : Confession was heard ; Benediction was given ; the Rosary was said ; and Fasts
and Feasts and Days of Obligation observed : but all
this was not sufficient inducement for us to try to
reach Glory, so we must have something special—
a whipping up, say.   We were all astir now, all excited :
sermons appealed to us, and good Catholics visited
us and invited us to the Holy Mission.   Our priest
warned and threatened : the hardened sinner who
did not respond to this call and who neglected to
avail himself of the special graces attached to the
Mission—well, God was likely to cut him off and never
give him another chance.   How comes it that we
were so bad ?   How sluggish, perverse, ungrateful
we must have been !   In spite of Holy Mass, where
God Himself comes present, in spite of the Sacraments,

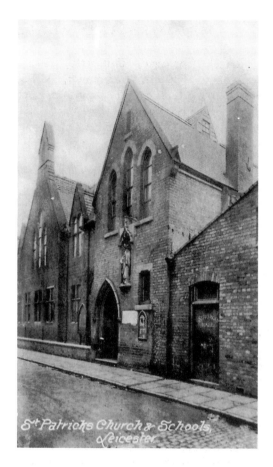

St Patricks Church & Schools Leicester

1824 saw the start of what was eventually to be St. Patrick's R.C.
Elementary School. A room was hired in Belgrave, with pupils being
taught where both in the daytime and the evening. This school was
enlarged in 1845. In 1852, the Catholic Poor Schools Committee (a
national body) remarked of Leicester that, "the erection of a new
schoolroom in a remote district, containing more than 200 children,
almost exclusively Irish, would meet the present deficiency, but there is a
want of funds". (5th report of 1852, p.90). In 1854 a new school-
cum-chapel, St. Patrick's, was built in Royal East Street. Barclay must
have been a pupil there.

St. Patrick's Church, Worcester, Interior.

The young Barclay and his family worshipped at St. Patrick's; he describes eloquently his own religious upbringing and the folk-religious beliefs of his Mayo-born mother.

(Interior and exterior photographs kindly supplied by Ms. Barbara Morris)

in spite of Our Blessed Mother's intercession, the
care of our guardian angels, and the prayers of the
Saints, we needed a Mission.

All that week of the Mission the back-sliders came
to chapel ; there were services every night, and we
imported an additional priest. He was eloquent, or
so we thought, and on one of the nights he preached
a sermon on Hell. If Love and Duty could not draw
us nor the prospective delights of Heaven, what
was there to do but threaten and frighten us ? The
new preacher, a Dominican, drew a lurid picture of
the torments of the dammed and their duration. If a
block of marble the height of a house were visited by
a bird every thousand years, and it were merely to
brush the block with its wing, the friction though
slight would in a great number of thousands of years
wear down the marble to a level with the earth, but
after the lapse of all that vast time, the torments of
the lost souls would be only commencing : and
bitterer than all the physical torment would be the
thought that they were separated from God for ever
and ever, and that they themselves by their own free
will had plunged themselves into that abyss. "Ah,
brethren listening here to-night, will you not while
there is yet time, and God's mercy and grace are
extended to you, will you not shun Hell and flee
from the wrath to come ? Will you not etcetera,
etcetera." The entire congregation was moved ;
some were evidently disturbed : nothing could be
heard but deep breathing and sighs : even the rows
of boys on the front benches were less restive than
usual. What fervent resolutions did we not make on

coming away, henceforth to lead different lives—
with the help of God really to renounce the Devil and
all his works, the World with all its pomps, and the
Flesh with all its temptations ! Some of us kept away
from the public house a whole fortnight, then we
began to backslide and slacken again. But I became
once more devout, and wanted to be learned. St.
Thomas Aquinas was my great pattern and I chose
him for my patron saint : I read somewhere in a
book that Our Lord Himself appeared to Thomas,
*The Great Ox of Learning, The Fifth and Universal
Doctor*, and said "Bene scripsisti de me, Toma ;
quam mercedam accipias ? " and Thomas answered
"Nil nisi Te, Domine." I'm not sure that my Latin's
correct, but I know the English of it is, "Well hast
thou written of me, Thomas ; what bounty shall I
bestow upon thee ? and the answer was "None, save
Thyself Lord ! " What a transcendent honour !
Complimented by Jesus Christ Himself ! Of course
it never occurred to me that whatever was meritorious
in Thomas's writings must have been inspired by
Jesus Christ—Who was God, and that it was rather
late in the day for Christ fourteen hundred years after
He established His Religion to get Thomas as amanu-
ensis and commentator to elucidate and make doctrines
plainer than they had been before. The whole
affair amounts to this "I am God, and I guide and
inspire you Thomas to write about Me : then I
personally thank you and want specially to reward
you for this thing that I am virtually author of and
writer of Myself." I assure any who may some time
or other read these contents that I feel no animus,

have no bias. I am simply bringing what intellect I possess to bear on the notions and credences that were poured into me before I had sufficient intellect to judge of them. Why should I be prejudiced, or quibble, or pretend ? How can one juggle with his soul ? Why have an intelligence if one cannot trust it ? I am just as sincere now that I believe in no creed as I was at the time of the Mission, and at that time I was transfigured. I felt we were all one great family with God for father and the Blessed Virgin Mary as dear mother. Our Father's Divine Will and presence were manifest : He was helping His children, and oh, what an unspeakable comfort ! What a sweet sense of joy and gratitude and safety and happiness for evermore !

I went to confession and communion monthly, and attended Novenas and Quarantores : I wore a blessed medal round my neck attached by a tape : I also wore the blessed cord of the Angelic Warfare. What's that ? you ask. Well, the legend is that St. Thomas Aquinas was sorely tempted to be unchaste, but successfully resisted all temptation, and then the angels appeared to him and girded him, and after that he was subject to no more temptation of that kind. I wore the girdle. The Church is very cunning : it does not make such observances articles of Faith, but it recognises and encourages them as means and instruments of Piety. If you want to know did the angels really gird St. Thomas you're told "Well, it's not an article of Faith :" at the same time, you may believe it if you like. This leaves the case undecided as to its truth or falsity. I had an aunt whose husband being a farm labourer in regular work enabled her to purchase a Douay Bible ; I paid frequent visits to the aunt and read that Bible from Genesis to the Apocalypse. Fancy going diligently through all that stuff of Leviticus and Numbers and Deuteronomy and Kings and so on ! Was it not, though, all the Word of God ? But some of the erotic incidents aroused my curiosity as to sexual matters. I had looked into Testaments and Bibles before, but they were not safe, being Protestant ones. The Douay version was the genuine thing. I read avidly whatever Church histories I could come across, and was greatly impressed with the decisions of the First Council of this and the Third Council of that. I learned something of the heresies of Arians, Nestorians, Berengarians, Pelagians and Donatists, and meandered through the meanderings of the Schoolmen. I remember my astonishment to find that members of the Greek Church were not Heretics, but only Schismatics. How strange though that their clergy are allowed to marry, and that even in the Roman Church at one time (I don't remember now when) priests took unto themselves wives ! This, after St. Paul saying it is not good for a man to touch a woman. The Church greatly honours the Blessed Virgin, but——well, a woman can be a nun, a canonized Saint, a Blessed Martyr, but she is barred from being a priest, or, if you will, priestess. The case of Louise Lateau brought confirmation to my faith : the age of chivalry might be gone, but the age of miracles was not. Louise was a Belgian peasant girl, a stigmatic, and about 1868 she was visited and examined and tested by medical men and pathologists from various countries of Europe. To do the Church justice, it stepped in even before the medical men to examine the remarkable phenomena. Louise became entranced and unconscious every Friday and bled from forehead, side, hands, and feet. I believe it was conclusively shown that the tests applied prevented the possibility of fraud. Everyone connected with the tests appears to have been puzzled. A question that occurs to me since is (supposing this to be intended for a Revelation) Why should a Belgian girl alone have this visitation that so few would become cognizant of ? Why not have visited or afflicted a dozen or a score girls similarly in every Christian country ? I had read of St. Francis of Assisi and other stigmatics of the past, but Louise's case was different ; the thing was taking place in our own day and before our very eyes.

From the time I was able to read at all, I wanted to know things ;—not necessarily to think and weigh,—that comes after : but I was interested in everything written about anything, and couldn't understand how most people seemed to be indifferent ; the disposition to learn is absent in them. What's to prevent a curious youth from learning something of Theology, Archæology, Mythology, Philosophy and Science, granted that he can obtain books ? *Milner's End of Religious Controversy* might satisfy my father and *The Life of St. Teresa* and *Think Well On't* my mother, but I had to go further, and so to my soul's ruin according to some, to my intellectual emancipation according to others. How well certain dicta stick in the memory after many years, as for instance, Macaulay on the Catholic Church,—"She may yet exist in undiminished vigour when some traveller from New Zealand shall in the midst of a vast solitude take up his stand upon a broken arch of London bridge to sketch the ruins of St. Pauls." And Cobbett saying of the Protestant Reformation "It was engendered in beastly lust, brought forth in perfidy and hypocrisy, and cherished and fed by plunder and devastation, and by rivers of innocent English and Irish blood." I couldn't help wondering how Cobbett and Macaulay could write such sentences without asking for admission into the Church. Ah ! if only I could write like the above authors ! But I discovered I needed Grammar and Logic and——no,—not Rhetoric.

> "For all a Rhetorician's Rules
> Teach nothing but to name his tools."

So I dropped that ; but Logic—I would have to be logical ; oh yes ; so I began to dabble with syllogisms, the undistributed middle, *ignoratio elenchi*, *sorites*, and the rest of it, and had no suspicion that James Thomson (B.V.) might be right when he says that logic is "the art of erring with method." Grammar of course was a *sine qua non*, and we must acquire it in the most hateful and foolish manner by learning all the rules and rigmarole of Orthography, Etymology, Syntax and Prosody. Wishful to be a poet as well as a prose writer and orator I must needs know something of Scansion too. Nietzsche hadn't yet arisen to condemn all this as useless and wasteful, so Bernard Shaw's contention held the field. Yes Shaw, you're right : if anyone needs grammar—correct expression —as a weapon in the war for social betterment, the proletaire is the one : dukes and lords and royalties might be slangy and slipshod in speech, but the King can say no wrong as well as do no wrong. The mere working class man must be precise and faultless in speech and in writing or he's turned down (or up) by everybody who is anybody as an uneducated ignoramus. So the way you say a thing is more important than the thing itself, and come on Lindley Murray, and Cobbett and Linnie ; come on so-and-so's Composition and Analysis. The pity of it ! Fifty times a day at my work in the factory I must hear such sentences as "It war im wat done it" and "I aint seed nowt on im" and at night at the Working Men's College I learn rules and find that the above sentences should be "It was he who did it" and "I haven't seen anything of him." "Words, words, words." *En arche en o logos* : it makes one almost believe it. What could be more ungrammatical than "me thinks" ? Yet this is a poetical diction, an't please ye. Pronunciation too was no little difficulty : I had to drop my Irish habit of rolling my "rs" and emphasising my "aitches" while at the same time avoiding the abominable Leicestershire *Eentche* ? for "Ar'nt you ? " *wick* and *ship* for week and sheep, *yow* for you and *ger* and *gor* for get and got. In the villages they actually say "street down that straight" for straight down that street. What could a foreigner make of "Giz" ? This is a contraction of "give us" and *us* is used instead of *me*, just as an editor says *we* instead of *I*. Is this what the philologists call a solecism ? I'm sure I've forgotten. Anyhow, don't think of learning a language from the uneducated.

A little way back I remarked that the disposition to learn is absent in some people : in the same way the disposition—or faculty—to distinguish between one sort of locution and another is absent in people. You can say to a shop-mate "I never knowed as 'ow he used to do a thatten" and "I never knew he used to do like that" and he'll understand each of them quite well, but apparently without finding any difference in them ; for myself, I never heard a sermon, or a lecture or address, but I noted grammar, pronunciation, terms and all the rest, and how it differed from ordinary usage ; I not only noted but I essayed to imitate ; the priest and the lecturer and the actor,—they were educated ; who else could be right ? The slightest difference of vowel pronunciation assails my ear, so that I want to locate the speaker : I notice, for instance, how the vowel "o" from being made with a shut mouth in Lancashire opens as you come down from the North until the mouth is wide open in Middlesex and the South. But enough of words and the expression of them; let's have a little more of thought and action *and* feeling.

Napoleon is credited with saying that the happiest day of his life was the day of his first Communion. I gladly acknowledge it was a happy day with me, but wait a bit. Nobody crosses you on that morn ; everybody is anxious to please you ; you're specially kissed and petted and washed and prepared, and a good breakfast is got ready for you as you come away from Mass fasting. Nobody scolded or flurried me all that morning or day that I took the Almighty God into my corporeal system. I remember playing snob-stones on the flagstone covering of the cistern

in our yard—the only flat space there was anywhere
about—and everyone was nice and smiled on me,
and all went merry as a marriage bell. Yes, I was
very happy : but how much soul or mind or greatness
or goodness could there be in the little chap who
delighted in a game of snobs the morning that he had
absorbed the body, blood, soul, and divinity of Jesus
Christ Who, being One with the Father, is the
Creator of the Universe ? Still, I'm glad, Mother,
that it pleased *you*, and made you feel happy on that
morn. It was not so long though after this that I did
things, or thought about things, that made me
ashamed to go to my ordinary confessor, and I went
out seven miles away to Ratcliffe-on-the-Wreake and
confessed to one of the Fathers of Charity. I went
now regularly to Sunday School and joined the
Choir. I don't know how ever we managed with but a
harmonium to sing Mozart's Twelfth Mass at Easter,
but we did. Boys and girls were both allowed to join
the Choir, and here I fell in love. Love takes no
notice of whether you are rich or poor, stupid or
intelligent, healthy or unhealthy, believer or unbeliever, but only are you young and sexually fit. The
last factor and requisite is the least to be put in
evidence however by this wily Potency, for nothing
could be farther from any gross bodily feeling and
idea than the sweet entirely spiritual transfiguration
called Love. I saw her at Mass—"It is engendered
in the eyes"—I saw her, and I was no longer what I
had been before. I can consider *now* that she was
nothing much out of the common—but *then*, Oh
ye Gods ! I was but a child of twelve as I came out
from Mass unable to take my eyes off her. I walked

carefully, timidly, some paces behind the Radiance.
I was too shy to accost the peerless being, much less
to joke or take any liberty. I had seen Polly before,
I think, but—whatever had happened ? She wasn't
the same at all, and I wasn't the same. I was fascinated,
and at the conclusion of the evening service—
Benediction—followed her on her way home. But
she loitered and deviated, and I had to loiter and
deviate as well. 'Twas the lodestone and the needle :
I wondered where she dwelt, and what and who she
was. Presently, in Lee Street, I heard a woman's
voice evidently accosting her roughly "Now then,
where have you been, I should like to know ? Off
you go to bed, my lady, and quick, before I help you."
Was it possible to talk to a Goddess like that ? How
irreverent, how shocking! What insensibility! Not
many moon's emitted their effulgence—you'll excuse
the poetic vein won't you ?—ere she was spirited
away whither I might not follow, namely, to Nottingham the boastful : but not before "she knew that my
heart was darkened by her shadow." Love and hunger
are diseases that cannot be concealed, says an Irish
proverb, and her girl-pals quickly discovered and
used mockingly to remind me that nothing she said
or did could I possibly find fault with.

And now came a crisis. I had a few raspy words
with father (I'm too respectful and antiquated to say
"the old man"), and I left home. Truly it was time
one or more of us moved with six sleeping in a room
nine feet by nine : there were tears, idle tears, but I
tore myself away with my violin which I soon broke
or sold, and went to lodge with Jem Dillon, the chap
I had borrowed Shakespeare from. I was now a bit

more comfortable but—I wish I had thought more about my mother. She sided with me—but—well, I was young and thoughtless. If she could appear to me now and know my thoughts and feelings, I'm sure she would be the first to forgive me, but for all that I cannot forgive myself. Thus the still small voice ; but there are two voices ; and the second one says "Don't worry ; your mother was no worse for you leaving home : she got a living as before, and don't you remember you were afraid if you gave her anything much it would only fall into father's hands and go in booze ? How do the old birds do when the young ones leave the nest and fly away ? The old ones live ; and didn't your father and mother try to "see life and enjoy themselves when they were young ? " This apologia somewhat calms me.

What was wrong ? Were there not enough material things "to go round" ? O Demiurgus, or Panturgus, or whatever god manages economics, what were you doing, pray ? Maybe you were asleep—or perchance you had gone on a journey. For if there had been full and plenty, what wrong could I have done ? Did I make myself and my natural desire to be decent and healthy and hearty ? "What is man that Thou art mindful of him ?" and echo answers "Beggared if I know ! " Furthermore, who made the nature of nearly all youths of the male persuasion, that instead of being saintly, or at least christianly free from vice, they are itchingly inquisitive—vicious to the core if there is any such thing as vice ? I haven't, Nietzsche, yet read your *Janseits Gut und Bose* but my little companions, Catholics too, mind you, were what conventionality calls "disgusting." Shall I skip the

sloughing period of adolescence, when one is struggling
out of boyhood into manhood, and feels as I suppose
a snake feels when casting his skin ? How distressing !
Probably the less frivolous and animalistic a youth is,
the more doubt throttles him till he wonders and
wonders whether he's normal—whether he's as other
youths are. Was there something deficient in me, I
asked myself, that I couldn't be like the youths of
my own age,—precocious, prurient, shameless, nasty ?
I was alone ; I was out of it. One can't associate with
old men, nor with mere babies, nor be entirely
apart and solitary. I suspected I was peculiar somehow,
because I was fond of reading, and was rather shy,
and timid, and unready—not at all smart and forward.
I was twitted with being pious, and laughed at as a
voteen (i.e., a devotee). Well, what is a youth going
to do who is naturally modest and pious and earnest ?
He's tempted to be a hypocrite and to make out that
he's like everybody else, and not so good as he really
seems. There are hypocrites who pretend to virtue,
but my young cockerel-pals pretended to vice : if you
didn't believe that they already consorted with
women, and were thoroughly capable of functioning
sexually they were ready to pull their coats off and
fight you. One more inconsistency : how square
this with the ideal of Perpetual Chastity, and the
singing of hymns celebrating the Purity of the
Immaculate Mother of God ? Am I too severe here ?
Mightn't the boasting and bravado of these young
fellows be simply begotten of the harmless desire to
appear manly ? Still, it looks like a case of "Not
Christ, but Barabbas": we did not want to be Patrick,
Dominic, or Francis ; give us Don Juan.

CHAPTER III.

MENTAL GROWTH AND CHANGE

AT the Working Men's College I attended classes under the Rev. D. J. Vaughan, Thomas Adcock, and George Newell. In the Rev. D. J. Vaughan's class we went right through Wordsworth's *Excursion* and Tennyson's *In Memoriam* ; I remember nothing now of the first, but some quatrains of the latter remain with me. Newell greatly encouraged and assisted me and was pleased when I obtained The Society of Arts certificate for English Language in 1875. Newell worked side by side with me at Cooper and Corah's, but he wasn't meant to remain there : he was one of the men who do things : he was mainly if not solely instrumental in forming the Leicester Co-operative Hosiery Society, and many think he came to an untimely end by undue anxiety and exertion. I wonder what I didn't read about this time—*Paradise Lost, Canterbury Tales, Pope's Homer and Essay on Man, Purgatory of Suicides, Ingoldsby Legends, Childe Harold's Pilgrimage,* and goodness knows what else.

Then behold me embarking on the Sea of Science. I believe it was at the same Cooper and Corah's Hosiery Factory that I made the acquaintance of George Robson. Robson was that *rara avis in terra,* the working-man scientist ; he didn't speak grammatically, and rather depended on me for a little polish in that direction, but he was an enthusiastic

naturalist and gave all his leisure time to the practical
study of Geology, Botany and Entomology. Specimens
of Leicestershire moths, butterflies, beetles and plants
collected by him will be found in our local museum.
Councillor F. T. Mott, and Joseph Dare the Unitarian
Missionary, were friends of his in the sixties. Many
and many a Sunday have we munched a cold dinner
together somewhere in Charnwood Forest—at Barrow-
on-Soar, or in Sheet-hedges Wood, or on Bardon
Hill. Robson would be equipped with vasculum and
net and cyanide of potassium jar, and the talk would
be of Belemnites, and Ammonites, and Gryphia
Incurva, and Crinoids, and Saurians, and Crypto-
gams, and Phanerogams, and Algæ, and Fungi, and
Lycopodiacœ ! What a way of spending the Sabbath !
But I was really glad when I got a certificate for that
horrifying science of Geology and could be done with
it. The butterflies and flowers were real poetry—
Puck and Ariel waving and fluttering ; but a geological
stratum or cutting is an ogreish funeral vault whose
dark, dead, silent hundreds of thousands of years
epoch paralyses the feelings. Laurentian, Cambrian,
Silurian, Devonian, Carboniferous, Triassic, Niassic,
Cretacious, Tertiary—Ach Himmel ! Iguanodons, and
Megalosaura

> "—— Dragons of the prime
> That tare each other in their slime."

and "the cheerful Pterodactyl"—shut them out
pray ! And I did, and went in for a little Physiology
and Biology instead. Let the dead past bury its dead :
get on with Hygienics and Economics. A shop-mate,
Bill Lee, with whom I lodged, and one of whose

daughters was afterwards married to the ex-Franciscan monk, Joseph McCabe, used to accompany me and Robson on our naturalistic rambles ; Bill was an ardent freethinker and a "good sort" but we never could agree on social questions, he being an unmitigated individualist.   My scientific studies did not prevent me from having a few drinks of beer and whisky, and from singing in pubs and at "Free and Easies," songs silly and songs humorous, such as "Judy Calligan," "Flannigan's Ball," "The Bold Militiaman," "Kitty of Coleraine," "I'm not Myself at all," "The Whistling Thief," and "Molly Carew." Some of these I am now ashamed of cos I'm different, but there's fun—innocent fun—in the last four.   I've also recited "Jabberwocky" and "The Baby's Debut" at the Secular Hall and elsewhere.   Ever from my youth up too have I gone in for tripping it on the light fantastic toe, and if you object to this in a thinker and philosopher we'll call up Nietzsche, and he'll slap me approvingly on the back and cry "Well done."   I taught a dancing class once for about six weeks at the Spiritualist Hall, Silver Street, and this was a brief joy for my intellectual sister Kate, who was one of my pupils.   These dances were all Waltz and Polka and Quadrille and Varsoviana, and so on, but later I reverted to things Irish, and *then*, nothing for me, thank you, but jigs and reels.   I took further certificates from the Science and Art department in Botany, Physiography, and Physiology,—but—what was there practical about it all ?   It's interesting I suppose to learn that a potato and a poisonous plant—the deadly nightshade, if my memory serves

me—belong to the same species, but you just tell a
practical gardener that and listen to what he'll say to
you. Ask him too what part of the potato plant the
potato is and you can't convince him that it isn't a
root. He'll have nothing to do with variations and
exceptions : the tuber may have "eyes" in it, but it
grows underground, ergo despite "eyes" or "nodes"
it's a root. Who's going to blame him ? I learned a
lot about the structure and functions of the body
without knowing that I suffered from indigestion, and
why : without knowing that a daily evacuation of
the bowels is a necessity if one wishes to be healthy.

I don't understand how a Catholic with any
intelligence much can read Darwin, Huxley, Tyndall,
Spencer, and such philosophers as Kant or Hegel
and remain a good Catholic. Perhaps he never reads
them, afraid of the devil. As for me, I knew I'd got the
very truth.   How could the arguments of Infidels
avail against the truth ? I felt I could discomfit them
and demolish them.   "So I did eagerly frequent 'discussions and debates and heard great arguments
about it and about, but didn't come out exactly' by the
same door wherein I went." Can it be that one who
is out to champion Truth and defend her shall be
overthrown and laid low by Infidelity and Error ?
What, out on behalf of God, and be defeated by the
Devil ? But I must say, instead of convincing, I began
to be convinced. All the thought and fact and evidence
seemed to be on the side of the sceptic and unbeliever,
and nothing was left the believer but his belief.
Thus, by using my intelligence on behalf of the Faith,
I found I should have to give up the Faith. It isn't

possible, it seems to me, for a Catholic (one of the Primitives, as Byron calls him) to become converted to any other Christian sect, but I was curious to see and know what was going on outside the Catholic pale ; so I visited Spiritualists, Mormons, Christadelphians and Unitarians, and became intensely interested in the creeds of Buddhists, Brahmins, Parsees, and Zoroastrians. I thought of the injunction "Go ye therefore and teach all Nations . . . . whatsoever I have commanded you." Where and when were and are the apostles and their successors doing it ? Statistics showed me hundreds of millions of Chinese, Burmese, Assamese, Siamese and Hindoos, and the testimony of travellers was that these were as earnest and as unshakeably fervent in their beliefs as we Christians in ours. Yet two thousand years would soon have expired without these vast populations, the majority of the civilized human race, having been converted. Millions of them, according to historians and anthropologists believed in religions older than the time of Abraham. "Before Abraham was I am" they each said. How possible not to begin to doubt ?

I took two more certificates : one for "Political Philosophy" under the Cambridge University Extension Scheme, teacher E. T. Cook (now Sir E. T. Cook, I believe), and one from the St. John's Ambulance Association : this last states that I'm qualified to render first-aid to the injured, but I pity anyone who might need me now after more than twenty-five years without a single patient. My sister said she was glad I had done something practical at last. But

I did something else practical. My father having gone the way of all flesh, I went back home, and took mother out of the rag-and-bone warehouse to keep house for me. She was not satisfied, however, simply to do that, and turned the front room into a second-hand clothes shop. The books I had to study to obtain my Political Philosophy certificate showed me the state of the ancient world, especially Greece, and I asked "Why should only one in six people in Athens of old be free and the other five slaves?" Then I began to study a little Political Economy, and came across such books as Henry George's *Progress and Poverty*, Max Nordau's *Conventional Lies of Civilization*, Carruther's *Communal and Commercial Economy*, and Ruskin's *Unto this Last*. I wonder who Carruthers is—or *was*; I don't know whether he's alive or not or anything about him, but the book seems to me truly revolutionary. But Draper's *Conflict Between Religion and Science* made a finished sceptic of me. What a book!

Dear mother, what a kind shrewd practical woman you were, and not without some ability to think for yourself on certain matters theological. You were a bit heretical on the subject of Predestination, but as the Church never discovered it, and you were not aware of it yourself, I don't think there's much the matter. You sometimes put me a poser, as when I was contending that Original Sin wasn't just, or that all sin was sin against man, not against God. You asked "Do you know better than all the saints and sages and Holy Fathers of the Church from its foundation down?" I was rather puzzled and a bit

too modest to say that I did, and yet——Ah, I used
to pain you, mother, I know I used ; but what could
I do ? You wanted to know why I no longer went to
Mass and to "my duty." How could I reveal to mother
the disbelieving state of my mind, how explain why I
had given up the Faith as a tissue of superstitions
and inconsistencies ? These were to her the only
great realities. My fears and struggles and doubts
and all a fervent Catholic would necessarily go
through in the process of becoming an Infidel—how
explain them ? Still, I had to criticise. When she
announced that the priest had requested the prayers
of the congregation for some one of the flock who
was seriously ill, I remarked that it struck me as
presumption : that God surely knew best whether
He wanted the person to be ill or not. Then it was
"Musha God help me this blessed day listening to
you ! I'm sorely afraid my boy that the Evil One, bad
luck to him, has got hold of you. It's all the fault of
this unfortunate country ; I wish I had never set
foot in it." "The inhabitants are all God's children,
mother, aren't they ? " "They are ; but they're
astray since Luther and Calvin and King Harry and
all that breed. Are you comparing yourself with the
heretics that have nothing but the light of rayson to
guide them with their blind guides ? 'They shall
both fall into the pit.' I hope and trust your sisters,
that are listening to you, won't take after you. Beware
of the sin of pride, my boy ! By that sin fell the
angels, and the Devil is very subtle." "Well I don't
see that he *is* so subtle ; if he's such a cunning fellow
as they make out, how came he to be such a fool as

to put himself up against the Almighty ? " "Oh,
you'll know all about it when you get as far as him,
you'll have a different tune then. Wait till you get
above."   'Twill be seen that mother's view was
anthropomorphic. Earth was perhaps a globe, but
certainly Heaven that eye hath not seen was spread
out flatly above the clouds, something like Swift's
floating Island of Lapanta only so much vaster ; the
floor of gold and the gates of jasper is it ? And
harpers harp on their harps, and angels are continually crying. After all, was she any more anthropomorphic than the Bible itself—or more inconsistent?
"Eye hath not seen ;" yet Paul is caught up and sees ;
and St. John saw a great deal if the Apocalypse is
canonical. But when I showed you that illustration
from *La Bible Amusant*, mother ! The illustration was
copied into G. W. Foote's journal *The Freethinker* and
showed Jesus walking on the water with a pair of
little canoes under Him, one on each foot.

"Oh then, may God forgive them ; and He has
great patience that He doesn't strike them dead,
and they to be mockin' Him like that. May the
Blessed Mother of God help me, and 'twas she
that rightly knew what a mother's feelings are. The
thought that any of mine should be ever lost is enough
to drive me crazy."

"Don't mother, don't ! Aren't other children just
as precious in the sight of God as *your* children ?
Won't it matter about the souls of others, if only
the souls of your children are saved ? "

"Of course it'll matter, the Lord God save us all !
But isn't me own flesh and blood the nearest and

dearest to me ? What talk you have. But sure your head is being turned with the books. I wish I never saw a sight of them same books ; 'tis they that have ye ruined I'm afeared."

"You said last week it was the Devil."

"It's the same thing ; he's the one that inspires the books."

"You mustn't meddle with them mother."

"No, I'll not do that, but I wonder what I done wrong to the Almighty that He should punish me seeing that——"

"Get that all out of your head : it'll be all right at the finish. Look here ! Do you think that I'm a hypocrite—a fair question ? "

"Oh no Tom, you're not that."

"Very well then. It'll be all right at the finish I tell you. God isn't going to punish me for thinking as I do ; in fact I can't help it : I didn't make myself. He can't punish me for being mistaken, surely, if I am mistaken ; so don't you keep upsetting yourself. I know it'll all come right. It can't be that you think the Devil's got me because I'm using the reason God gave me : what has the Devil to do with that ? "

"I say, you're beginning to bore me with this old-fashioned mother of yours ; you said she was remarkable ; how do you show it ? "

"Who are you, pray ? And I didn't say remarkable, I said shrewd, practical."

"I'm the reader."

"I've got no readers ; don't want any."

"Oh dear, don't you ? You're kiddin'—I mean humbugging—yourself if you think you don't. There

never was a writer yet that didn't want readers :
wot's 'e got to write for if 'e don't ? "

"Well, anyhow, if my mother doesn't interest you,
leave her : she interests me."

There were two dishes she used to prepare, and I
wonder if they've become obsolete out of Ireland.
Potato cake was an amalgam of potatoes and flour
shaped like a pancake, cooked similarly, slit through,
and buttered. Cally, or callcannon (I must guess at
the spelling) consisted of milk and pounded potatoes.
Boil your tubers in their jackets ; skin them, shredding
them into an iron pot, then pound away with a
wooden rammer, adding milk as much as the potatoes
will hold. Then turn the pottage out on a plate,
scoop a hole in the middle, insert a lump of butter in
the hole, and eat, dipping your spoonful in the butter.
I think you'll like it, but let me say I think both this
and potato-cake tax the digestive processes.

She had a theory that nobody entered Heaven
from the Creation down before Christ. I don't know
how she got this tenet ; I've never seen it put forward
as Catholic doctrine, but it seems right and just,
meet and salutary. Man had forfeited all claim to
enter Heaven on account of the Fall : Heaven was
opened by the atonement of the Saviour. It was to
Abraham's bosom,—or "The Hell of the Holy
Patriarchs" as my mother called it, that the soul of
Christ descended during the three days that His
body was in the tomb. This, I take it, would be the
place Lazarus came forth from on being resurrected.
Since the advent of Christianity it has been re-named
Purgatory.

Isn't it a bold thing for an Irish person with a "brogue" mockingly to imitate what she considers bad English pronunciation ? Says mother, "I asked the woman with the stall of cabbages at the corner, were they chape, an she sez "My wench, we're a geein' on 'em awee ! " *id est*. We're giving them away.

"Did ye have tea in Ireland, mother, when you were a little un ? "

"Sorra dhrop of tay I ever dhrai k, or used to see till I don't know what age I was ; an' I was none the worse for it. Sure the English have the guts scalded out o' them with tay. Many's the healthy and happy day we had before ever we saw the likes of it."

"Were you good-looking when you were a young woman, mother ? "

"Troth and I was then : I had an eye that would coax a donkey from his oats." During the laughter which followed this reply in came Jem, the lodger, three sheets in the wind ; he wasn't staggering, but his talk was a little thick, and his eye was glassy. Mother regarded him pityingly. "I see yer looking at me Mrs. Barclay : oh, I know I've 'ad a drink, but I'll be a teetotaller yet." "You will when the Devil's blind, and he hasn't sore eyes yet." Jem went crest-fallen to bed, and I went to a meeting, and my sister told me on my return that mother had been deploring my state of mind. Comparing me with my brother and the lodger, she said "If it had been Jem, the boyo, or Martin, I wouldn't be surprised ; but to think that the only steady one I've got that I can rely upon to work, and come home quiet, and never get

into the hands of the police——ah well, let us pray
for him ! " "That's just what she said." Whereupon
I fell to parodying scripture, "Let one be boozer, a
shirker, a wife-beater, and a good-for-nought, and it
shall be forgiven him, but let him not think for himself ; for in the day that he presumeth to think for
himself he shall be surely cut off, and cast out utterly,
and the place that knew him once, shall know him
no more for ever. Selah ! "

I was now a constant reader of Free-thought Magazines and Journals such as *The National Reformer*,
The Freethinker, *Our Corner*, and *The Secular Review* ;
but neither the polemics of Charles Bradlaugh, nor
the erudition of John M. Robertson, nor the questionable sarcasms of G. W. Foote wrought half so effectively in the cause of Freethought as certain lectures by
Colonel Ingersoll. I read *The Gods, What must I do to
be saved ?* and *Some Mistakes of Moses* with keen
delight : the masses could understand these. I don't
now remember which one contains a criticism of the
Deluge, but I know I was laughing as I opened the
door returning home, and my sister, observing the
mischievous light of battle in my eye, said "For
goodness sake don't let's have another theological
discussion,—perhaps ending with a cry."   "No ;
perhaps you can put me right, mother, for *I* can't
answer some of the questions here, though they look
simple. The writer is a man named Ingersoll. He wants
to know, as to the Deluge, how eight people alone
managed to fodder and water and tend all those
animals ; there were thousands of them, you know.
What did the lions and tigers feed on, and how were

they prevented from killing the sheep and oxen : how were tropical animals kept warm enough, and how was it made cold enough for the seals and polar bears : he wants to know how fishes and whales and such went on, as all the water was outside ; whether adders, and scorpions, and boa-constrictors didn't bite and sting and do injury. He says there were tens of thousands of noxious reptiles and insects, and that we're not told anything as to how they were dealt with."

"Sure God's arm isn't shortened : couldn't the same Power that created them work a miracle to keep them in their places until the water subsided ? It bates me that if anything comes from science you're ready to believe it, but not if it comes from God or His Holy Church. Isn't that the truth now for ye ? But what can I do, asthor (oh treasure) but pray for you as the Blessed St. Monica did for her son, St. Augustin, until God turns you back to the Faith in His own good time." "All right, mother ! " My sisters told me afterwards that when I had gone out she said "Well then, talkin' of reptiles, and snakes, an' vermin, it's often I've wondered myself, God forgive me, why he should make rats and beedles (beetles) and bugs and flays to persecute us and annoy us as they do. But *don't, for the life of ye, say a word of this to Tom ! "*

A few nights after this, hearing my mother express a wish, as regards the Secular Hall, that she might never die until not one stone of it remained upon another, I made up my mind to play her a trick. I took her and my sisters to the Opera House to see

(and hear) *The Mikado*.   Mother was reluctant to
go, but she didn't like to refuse me—"payin' good
money to support idlers" she remarked in reproach-
ful tones. So we went, and all sat in the gallery, as I
begrudged pit prices. The only thing I remember
as regards mother's reception of the play is that
when Nanki Poo appeared, he having on a sort
of trunk hose or tights quite white in colour and,
extending from his middle to his shoes, mother
exclaimed "There he has a fine pair of legs for a
man, and no mistake ; but what in the name of
goodness made him white-wash them." On coming
out, I spoke to my sisters "Don't tell mother where
I'm taking her till after ; we'll go into the Secular
Hall Club." "Come on mother, we'll drop in at the
Hall of Science and have a drink." At the Secular
Hall I whispered to the manager and his wife not to
let up on me as to mother's whereabouts. She was
made very welcome, and had a nice drop of Irish
whisky. At that time the Secular Club had a bar
open for the sale of alcoholic drink to its members
and their friends : Mr. F. J. Gould had not yet come
among us. Mother admired the grand place with its
books and pictures and spacious tables, and thought
the members very nice people : it was not until a
week after that my sisters informed her that the
place she was praising was the Secular Hall.

"*Musha, ye don't say so* ! Well, well, look at that
now ! But I'll be even with Tom for this."

I'm in the habit when I go a country walk, of having
a book in my pocket,—the which I pull out and
read as I go along. Even when taking my ease in

mine Inn, I have the cheek sometimes to pull it out and read a bit : then there are nudgings and surprised stealthy looks and mutterings. At times I've been addressed with a friendly slap on the shoulder, something like this. "Ah, if I'd only got an eddication like you, I wouldn't be where I am, I can tell you." After a little palaver, I've gathered that my friend believed his financial status would be much improved if only he had "book-learning." Riches followed in the wake of Literature and Learning : these had no value in themselves, mind you, but they enabled you to get money. What an' estimate ! What's the good of History or Art or Philosophy unless they get you money ? But I say unto all mere proletaires who want to "get on," Don't imagine books will help you. Let them alone, and try more profitable methods. Don't desecrate Learning by attempting to make it the drudge and handmaid of commercialism. I've been called a Book-worm. Well, I'm just going to retaliate. I'm a book-lover, and I want to know were we sent into life only to make money ? Learning is meant to better life, to increase it, to extend it. What is money meant for ? I know a fellow who years ago worked beside me in the factory as a young man, he pushed and worried and scraped and scrambled : he bred fowls and rabbits and swopped this thing and the other : he gave all the energies of his prime, early and late, to heaping up shekels. Well he's got 'em, a thousand pounds or so I should think : but he's got nothing else, and he might have failed to get the shekels after all his struggling and striving : some do. He's to-day a heavy-footed ignoramus, whose god is his belly. Do you think I'd exchange the little I know for his thousand pounds and be a dunce and a dunderhead ? I'm living fifty lives in one ; whereas he's not living the *one* rightly in my opinion. I'm living right back in Ancient Egypt and Chaldea and Assyria. I'm in Central America among Aztecs and Toltecs hundreds of years before Columbus discovered it. I'm acquainted with Aristophanes the satirical and Euripides the human——Oh dear ! As George Robey says "Desist, desist ! " But what except the crassest ignorance, in spite of all the geniuses that have lived poverty-stricken lives, in spite of Grub Street, in spite, in recent times, of Evylin Douglas, Francis Adams, James Thomson (B.V.), George Meredith and George Gissing, would lead anyone to think that Learning and Literature would bring money. Not in *this* country, sirrah, is Learning likely to get you cash ; there's no market for it, and generally we ignore it : sometimes we actually despise it. I worked some twenty-five years ago in Wellingborough at Walker and Kempson's shoe factory : one of the Managers, one Harry Sursham, got me on there. I found in Wellingborough no Free Library, and no love of anything but Boxing and Gambling and Football. I believe nearly every inhabitant of that place got a considerable amount of drink on Saturday nights : but that can be pardoned : what I couldn't pardon was the contempt I found expressed for books and learning. I was considered a noodle. How different are the Irish ! I won't say anything about the Scottish, for everyone acknowledges they are brainy. But take the Irish : if they are not cultured themselves, they look up to, ay, and almost reverence, anyone that is. I rather think the Welsh are the same. Now Mr. So-and-so "wat don't know nowt," listen to this. "In the high honour paid to Learning the Chinese teach us a lesson. The lowest among them can rise to the highest offices in the State, these being given, not to the best born, but to those who have passed with the greatest merit the public examinations; so that knowledge is the road to power." Ah, you didn't know, did you ? You've been used to your abominable caricature of a pig-tailed, yellow-skinned Ching-Chang Chap. But who's my authority ? I'll tell you :—Edward Clodd, in his book on *The Child-hood of Religions*, and I think he knows what he's talking about : he daren't give bigoted Christians a chance of convicting him of a mistake.

During the Great War that began in 1914 I worked at a certain Dye Works, I have worked at quite twenty factories in Leicester during the last fifty years, but the lot of men who worked there were the worst I ever sampled. There was a hustling bustling chap, said to be an "American," a specialist worker in something ; there were three or four men, since dead, on the verge of imbecility but not lacking muscle ; their shoulders stooped, their mouths hung, and they shambled in their walk, but they had muscle : there was a malignant humbug who watched and dodged the managers and shirked all he could, and a patient honest rather old man victimised into doing more than his share through the shirking of the malignant ; a sycophantic crawler ready to put up with anything, and a man who, it was said, had been a manager and seemed anxious to be one again. These are a few specimens of from seventy to eighty hands who sneered at one another, barged one another, and worked *against* instead of in harmony *with* one another. Managers sauntered and prowled, but seemed unable to distinguish between the humbugging shirkers and the straightforward hands who were doing their best. Now and then, one of the "heads" moved about, silent, rigid, smileless, aloof ; no vizier or czar could be more distant and important-looking : he seemed less happy than any workman there who was earning him profit. Poor rigid, frigid head ! Poor herd of robots and yahoos ! Why do I mention this place, where I found only three rational social sensible fellows ? Just to compare it with the reasonable place I'm employed in at present. At the Dye Works there were few Trades Union hands : where I am at present, the manager himself encouraged and assisted the hands to join the Union. Where I am, manager and men talk to and chaff one another : no starchiness, no caste, no man walking up and down idle, spying on us to see that we swink well ; and we do our best nevertheless, and do it ungrudgingly : we feel that we'd rather help the Firm than do anything to hinder it. How different from a shoe-factory, where, I'm told, a man sits, or stands on a raised platform that he may see if any leaves his work for a moment to speak a word to another. Where I am we laugh and joke and smoke and shout and sit a minute or two, and then we get our work done. If any new-comer tries to shirk, we shame him out of it, and bring him to book. You've got to get men's hearts in their work to get the best out of them, but *this* the capitalists are too silly to see.

At the aforesaid Works I was but a casual hand, a dyer's labourer, an old man. Well, the dyers who were Trades Unionists, obtained an advance in wages, and that made some of the rest of us discontented. We began to agitate, and the heads of the firm came to hear of it and summoned one of the ring-leaders.

"You've been trying to get the men to join the Union" said a "head."

"Yes," said the ring-leader, "I believe in a living wage, and we're not getting it."

"Do you know what we do with hands that agitate like that ? "

"You can do what you like, Sir ; if you sack me I can get another place, and my Trade Union 'll defend me till I do."

The "hand" didn't get the sack, but how slowly we move ! Slavery, Serfdom, Diggerism, Chartism, Socialism—how slowly we move ! The slave,—wage-slave or otherwise, does not know he is such. If he learns that he is, and becomes a rebel, what support does he get from his fellow-slaves ? Some are con-centrated on "the next world," saving their souls : some are absorbed by trivialities, Football, Cricket, and Horse-racing ; you'ld think they must be capitalists and millionaires : and some are breaking their hearts and risking their health in desperate efforts to cease being proletaires and to rank themselves among the capitalists.

Why should I eat my heart out like poor Barbellion

or Marie Bashkirtseff ?   I shall never do as much
in Literature as that pathetic and lovable deaf, dumb
and blind woman, Helen Keller, the eighth wonder
of the world as I think Mark Twain called her.   But
what necessity is there ?   What would I be at ?
Fiction ?   Hasn't Thomas Hardy written ?   Haven't
George Meredith, George Moore, and George Gissing?
I argued a quarter of a century ago that there were four
novelists in England who were head and shoulders
above all others then living—a Thomas and three
Georges : and who reads them ?   Not the readers of
Marie Correlli and Ethel M. Dell.   I'ld rather be
the author of *The Way of All Flesh* than of all Rider
Haggard ever wrote, though *She* was acclaimed of the
critics and underwent fourteen editions in one year.
I'm reminded of such frothy songs as "Bubbles"
that are chuntled by everybody for a short season and
then deservedly die.   Who now reads Haggard ?
And what are the ones who read him and liked him
now reading ?   Why *Tarzan of the Apes*, I suppose.
When I was a child I read like a child, *Nick Carter*
and *Deadwood Dick*, but when I became a man I
wanted *Fathers and Sons* and *Madame Bovary* and
Wilhelm Meister and *Germinal*.   I'ld like to write a
good play, but can I do anything like Hauptmann, or
Gorkie, or Galsworthy, or Ibsen, or O'Neill, or
Bernard Shaw ?   I think not.   Very well ; so be it.
Peace, my soul !   You can love these authors, worship
them, bless them.   Let that much go on record, somewhere, sometime,—that I, unable to do anything
great myself, did the next best thing : I prized and
loved the greatest and best.   Come on, Joyce—

"Portrait of the Artist as a Young Man." Come on
Mac Gill—"The Ratpit." Come on Mackenzie—
"Sinister Street." I clasp ye to my bosom : ye are
with me, and I with ye. Glorious fellows all !

It seems far back in another life that I joined *Les
Bons Enfants.* We were a party of seven or eight who
wanted to know French, and to speak it. What
aspiring youth is there that doesn't wish to know
French ? We had a Frenchman among us, one Gasper
Martin, and an Italian, and met either in a tavern,
or on an allotment garden on the Belgrave Road. The
whole space between Dorset Street and the Belgrave
turn was, about 1885, occupied by gardens. I soon
picked up a little French in the company of speakers,
getting hold of the pronunciation for the first
time after many attempts in reading classes. I wanted
to read Victor Hugo and Zola in the original, but I
did not persevere. I wonder if the latter was put on
the Roman Index Expurgatorius like his countryman
Anatole France.* What a series it is, the Rougon
Macquart series ! I have read most of them, but
mostly in English, I remember the tirades of abuse
evoked in the English Press, and the accusations of
obscenity and filth. But a certain American critic's
utterance struck me as the most arresting and thoughtful. Not that Zola described vileness and badness
was worth considering, according to this critic, but
whether the vileness and badness really existed.
Was Zola calumniating his country men and women,
or only telling the truth, exposing their corruptness ?
If a malodorous drain or cesspool is discovered in

* Yes, he was.

our midst, is it better to deal with it and remove it, or to cover it up and pretend that it is not there ? And surely, if an author describes vileness, it doesn't follow that he is vile in himself. What *is* vileness, or indecency, or immorality in a writer ? If it can be maintained that the author of the *Decameron* is immoral and entices to vice because his tales are palatable, then Zola is profoundly moral and deters from vice, for he makes vice shocking and disgusting. Let us not forget that the same mind that produced *Nana*, produced *The Dream*, and *The Ladies' Paradise*. *Human Brutes* and *The Soil* are a deal filthier, a deal more horrible than *Nana*, while *The Dream* is pure and sweet, and *The Ladies' Paradise* romantic and optimistic. My own favourite is *Germinal*,—I suppose because I am a rebel and a Socialist.

I've often wondered how it is that priests and Doctors of Divinity and those, whoever they are, that have to read Zola and Anatole France before they can condemn them, never get contaminated themselves. To put some objectionable author on the Index I must first read him, but his words do no injury to a high ecclesiastic like me, bless you ! Oh no ; it's the laity, the common people that are likely to be injured. I am forgetting though, that clerical readers may perhaps fortify themselves by some special . grace obtained through prayer and fasting.

I have at different times been a member of four or five Clubs, including the Secular Club, and an Irish National Club : two of these called themselves Labour Clubs, but they did precious little for the cause of Labour. This was not the fault of the founders,

who were men full of high hopes for something other
than beer and skittles. I don't believe in what somebody wrote, that

"They who taste the smallest drop of liquor alcoholic
Are doomed as sure as eggs are eggs to torments diabolic."

But if a Club is simply a place for beer and bagatelle,
cards and comics, then it shouldn't to its primary
title append the words—"and Literary Institute." I
must say, on behalf of myself, whenever I've found
them to forget and ignore the Literary part, I've drawn
out.

We have at the present time—November, 1924—
several large and well-patronised clubs in Leicester :
they could, one has to think, be a tremendous
influence towards the understanding and solving of
social problems, but they are not. I leave the definitely
political clubs, such as the Liberal and the Constitutional, out of the question ; but we have among
others the Aylestone, the Belgrave, the Asfordby
Street, the Manchester, and the Bond Street, and in
not one of these is there such a thing as an educational
class, lecture, or debate. I dare say some have tried.
I've been to a lecture at Bond Street Club, but there's
no such thing now : I suppose the thing was attempted
and fell through. You'ld think that, as we're not, the
bulk of us, livers on dividend and rent and interest—
merely idlers living on what others produce,—we
would have *one* night a week, at least, devoted to
Economics and Sociology ; but not so : we're just
like those that live out of us,—simply thinking of
nothing but how to waste the time and to amuse
ourselves. Horse-racing, Football, Sports—these are

of primary importance, and we discuss them in and
out of factory and workshop, whereas Social Problems
are considerably second—or nowhere.   What   a
bitter but true saying that of yours, Bernard Shaw,
that if it were not for the working man we would
have had Socialism established long ago.   What
could keep the masses out of it if they really wanted it
and went for it ? And how ashamed they ought to be
that middle-class men like H. G. Wells, Sidney Webb,
and Bernard Shaw fight their battles, while they
themselves remain inactive !

To-day, we have no Labour Club in Leicester ; I
suppose we've learnt that we'ld get no proper support
of one unless we sold intoxicants, and that if we *did*
sell intoxicants there would be little interest in
anything else. I remember the first Labour Club—
the Bedford Street one—of some thirty years ago,
and the great hopes we had of it. I myself taught a
class there and solicited and obtained gratis an entire
set of Ruskin's works from Mr. Paddy Logan, for the
use of the members. Well, the Club degenerated, and
finally became extinct—died of booze, I suppose, like
the Working Men's Club of Vine Street that was
nick-named "The Flea-pit." Does anyone remember
Labour Club No. 2, of Millstone Lane ? That also
went down, and I suppose for similar reasons.   It
was at No. 2 that a discussion took place one night
which passed from affairs of this world to affairs of
an assumed other one. Two or three Catholics were
present and during the discussion one of them said
to me "I'd like to ask you, Tom, one question. Are
you any happier now you're a Freethinker than when

you believed ? " I replied "I believe, all things considered, I *am* happier, I used to have religious exaltations now and then when a Catholic, but I also had times of great gloom and anguish—the feeling that God was forsaking me—and—don't you chaps think I haven't lived through what somebody calls 'the night of the soul.' When I began to doubt, I was sore afraid to doubt, for fear it might be the work of the Devil. I believed as long as ever I could : I took my doubts to the priest, but he could only tell me to pray that my doubts would be removed. I was doing that. The poor fools that have tried to bully me for renouncing 'The Faith' little know what I had to pass through. How can a man juggle with his soul ? He simply can't. But I got clear of the superstition that God was allowing the Devil to tempt me and damn me ;—and in fact, if you'll allow me the mixed metaphor—Hell flames was the rock on which I split. I came to feel convinced that the Devil himself would never torment his worst enemy in Hell for ever and ever, and how could God be worse than the Devil." After further talk another Catholic said to me "Have you read *The Lives of the Saints*, Tom ? " "Yes," I answered, "I have, and you won't hear me say a word against them, unless they're bigoted ; why should I ? Francis, and Catherine of Sienna, and Francis Xavier, and Teresa ;—but there are Brahminical and Buddhistic Saints too. The Trappist monk's fastings and scourgings can't compare with those of a Hindoo Fakir. I look at all religions as attempts to explain the Mystery of Being—the meaning of Life—why we're here, and what we ought to do, and what's going to become of us—the meaning of it all. I chose Thomas Aquinas, the Angelic Doctor, for my patron saint on account of his reputed great Learning, but I've done with him. What do you think he says : you'll find it in Part Three of the *Summa* : he says '*Beati in Regno Celesti videbunt paenas damnatorum ut beatudo illis majis complaceat.*' That means that the happiness of the Blessed in Heaven will be increased by watching the torments of the damned ! You'ld think the most hardened murderer—the most insidious poisoner— would hardly announce such a thought, if he were hellish enough to think it. Contrast the sentiment with that expressed by the pessimistic poet James Thomson,

> If any human soul at all
> Must die the second death, and fall
> Into that gulf of quenchless flame
> * * * *
> Then I give God my scorn and hate,
> And turning back from Heaven's Gate,
> (Suppose me got there) bid "Adieu
> Almighty Devil ; damn me too."

This was, of course, revolting to the Catholics, who soon retired, though without anger. Whereupon one of the other disputants said to me "They've stood it well for Catholics, Tom." "You're right," said I, "it shows rather exceptional intelligence in a Catholic that he's willing to discuss such things at all."

CHAPTER IV.—SOCIALIST PROPAGANDA

I BELIEVE I am to-day (July 17th, 1925, and the seventy-third anniversary of my birth) the oldest Socialist in Leicester. I'm the oldest living Leicester propagandist, anyhow. "Ancient History" you will say. I once heard George Jacob Holyoake discourse in a room over some stables at the back of where the present Secular Hall is built : there was no Secular Hall, then. Later I heard the Chartist Leader, Thomas Cooper, after his conversion to Christianity, speak, criticising Darwinism in Friar Lane Chapel. About 1880 I went in for a course of Economics, or Political Economy as it was then called : my books were by Adam Smith, J. S. Mill, and somebody named Marshall. But I soon threw over the Manchester School after reading *Progress and Poverty* by Henry George, *Communial and Commercial Economy* by Carruthers, *The Co-operative Commonwealth* by Gronlund, *Unto This Last* by Ruskin, and something or other by Belfort Bax. Mullhall and Giffen's Statistics also greatly influenced me. Up to this the progressives amongst us, even the Secularists, appeared to be all radicals. Chartism was dead, and no one knew anything of the Socialism of the times of Robert Owen. Many thought the abolition of Royalty would put us all right. To give the Secularists their due, they were never afraid of the fullest discussion of the most adverse ideas and criticisms : they welcomed criticism, but they began to strike me as people who, renouncing superstitions relating to belief in another life, clung to superstitions that ought to have been long enough regarded as exploded in this. About 1883, the Bradlaugh *v.* Hyndman debate in St. James's Hall, London, inclined many thoughtful people to Socialism. Some of Bradlaugh's right-hand adherents left him soon after :—Mrs. Besant, and Dr. Aveling, to wit. The Fabian Society sprang up and the Secular Society was the first in Leicester to invite their speakers and expounders. We listened here to the seven whom J. M. Robertson styled "The Seven Against Society"—the Fabian Essayists :—amongst them were Sidney Webb, Hubert Bland, Mrs. Besant and Bernard Shaw.

It may surprise a good many to learn that the first Socialist paper published was a little thing called *The Christian Socialist* ; it was, I believe, edited by the Rev. Stewart Headlam. Soon followed *Justice*, and soon after that (there being some disagreement between William Morris and H. M. Hyndman) *The Commonweal*. And now we began to meet—"we few against the world"—to address the "many-headed monster thing" from trolley platforms in all the different squares in Leicester. Every Sunday twice, and sometimes two or three week-nights. We preached and exhorted : we formed classes : we sold literature : we challenged opponents : we held debates: we collected coppers to pay the train-fare of speakers from other towns, and among these were Kate Conway (Mrs. Bruce Glasier), Tom Mann, J. N. Mahon, Charley Mowbray, George Cores, Fred Charles, Tom Maguire, Clynes the present Government official, Frank Kitz, D. J. Nichol, Prince Kropotkin,

William Morris, Halliday Sparling, Cunningham Graham, Enid Stacey, and Countess Schaak. I suppose there were similar little groups in other large towns, zealous, enthusiastic, confident, filled with the fire of faith, self-effacing pioneers and apostles, reckless of whether they could leaven the lumpy-minded lump, uncalculating as to how many swallows it takes to make a summer. Neither blame them nor praise them ; they acted as the wind bloweth. Ought I to say they, instead of we ? We annihilated all the arguments of Teetotallers, Co-operators, Malthusians, and Individualists like Auberon Herbert and W. H. Mallock. I had discussions in the Press on Socialism *versus* the Present System, and among my opponents were Revd. Martin Anstey, Revd. F. B. Meyer, and Revd. J. Page Hopps. Remarkable isn't it, that Christian Ministers should oppose us ? And how did they manage to agree with the Christian Socialists?

Do you laugh cynic ? I'm not sure but you have cause. Were Christian Ministers guarding their loaves and fishes—and therefore hand-and-glove with the well-to-do people who kept them in their snug positions, or were they as honest as ourselves ? Remember, *we* were accused of only wanting to upset the existing system for selfish and sordid reasons. Good argument, wasn't it, poor stupid uncompre-hending listener ? We'd got nothing, so we were envious of those who had something, and were out to despoil and dispossess. That settled it for you, I suppose. You couldn't have understood us, surely, or you would have stood up with us ; *you* had nothing to be despoiled of, anyway. Yes, it must have been your stupidity—that quality which men and gods fight against equally in vain. Why, if ye could think, ye'ld know that any of us who were out for self could have got it much easier by standing up *against* ye, and as Conservatives, Liberals, or Individualists defending the unjust system that produced ye.

"Look at So-and-so ; *he's* got on ; it's grit that does it."

"You want enterprise, and thrift, and you never know your luck."

"Why shouldn't a man make a bit, eh ? "

"So-and-so started wi' next to nowt ; now 'e's got thousands. Good luck to 'im ; we *must* 'ave *capital*. Wish I were in 'is place ; wouldn't you do the same if ye could ? Course ye would ! "

"How is it wrong to make profit ? You wouldn't go into business unless you could make a bit o' profit out o' somebody, would ye ? Why, if ye only keep a bit of a stall in the market ye want to make a bit o' profit, don't ye ? ",

You could see all this, poor dear proletarians, but you couldn't see when So-and-so after saving and striving and denying and at length opening his little shop, failed and became bankrupt, that company promoters, and syndicates, with their immense capital had anything to do with causing it. Oh no : he was unlucky, that was all. The whole industrial system visualised itself to you as a gigantic Monte Carlo ; business was a game, and some were bound to lose. You had no notion that Society could be a com-munistic co-operative organisation :—that a rich man with his villas and hunting-grounds, and cooks and

butlers and footmen and ladies' maids and jewellers
and yacht-builders and deuce knows what,—that all
these were parasitic and unproductive and a sheer
heavy burden on Labour ; that all their wealth, both
necessaries and luxuries, was due to Labour—owing
to a disguised system of robbery of Labour. What the
good of telling you that the slums of Denman Street,
Brook Street, Metcalf Street, Eaton Street, and Carley
Street ought not to exist in any really civilized society ?
Why couldn't you compare the worse than pig-styes
of Bedford Street and Brittania Street with the
stately villas and spacious grounds of Stoneygate ?
Servants you didn't want, but you could have done
with ventilation and space and a pleasant site and
comfortable beds and furniture, and better food and
more leisure. "Oh, well, it would never run to it,"
you say, "we couldn't all have mansions and grounds."
Then if only some can have them, have those who've
got them got them by their superior personal merit ?
How can that be when we find them non-producers
of wealth, parasites who make no goods—never put
a hand to anything ? Oh, but I forgot ; it's owing to
luck, and—yes, to gambling. Even regarding things
as a gamble, we tried to show you that the dice were
loaded against you from the start—that the race was
sold—that not one in a thousand of you ever had a
ghost of a chance to win aught but to live in slums
and work hard (when you could get it) and to die in
poverty. We tried to show you Tavern-keeper, and
bank-clerk, and overseer, and editor, and every class
other than you, seemingly arrayed against you,
anxious to keep you where you were, because that

allowed them to be where they are. But you couldn't
understand, or (astonishing thing) you had no
disposition to understand. Poor, perverse, up-side-
down lot of fools ! We showed you that the land was
thieved from you, that it could no more be made
than the air you breathed, and therefore it should be
common to all, like the air. We proved the immorality
of Interest, a thing that allows a millionaire, though
getting only two and a half per cent. on a million, to
spend twenty-five thousand pounds yearly and still
have his million. All to no purpose. You were blind
to the parasitism and uselessness of titled aristocrats,
sinecurists, ambassadors, stock-brokers *et hoc genus*,
but if one of your own class who had agitated on
your behalf got into some office, instead of rejoicing
you were mean enough and unjust enough to suspect
and to hint that he had had an axe to grind. I feel
like saying damn you ! or at least like washing my
hands of you : but if I did that, my Socialism would
be "gone glimmering thro' the realm of things that
were." I have been working and hoping these last
thirty-five years for a new and better state of things,—
a something that isn't required by any class but yours.
We believed in Heaven on Earth as fervently as ever
the Religionist believes in a Blessed State of Im-
mortality. But stay : have I any right to feel like
damning you ? No ! I withdraw. I am of your class,
and we must go together, sink or swim : if you want
nothing better than what you have, so be it. I said
that we agitators showed you this, and proved to you
the other, but am I sure that you ever understood us ?
What does good old Walt Whitman say ? "Do I

contradict myself ? Very well, I contradict myself."
Something like that. We were accused of being
"young men in a hurry." God knows, or He ought
to do, it was high time somebody hurried a bit over
certain things. Perhaps we were in a hurry : we had
read Omar Khayyam. We wanted to be able to go
to the Riviera and to Madeira. We wanted to hear
Melba and Tetrazini and Joachim and Paderewski as
well as the classes that never worked. I suppose those
who accused us of being in a hurry belonged to the
parasitic exploiting class, who could go to those places
whenever they chose, and hear those artists. Did I not
say that it was your class—my own class—that we
were out to better ? Anyhow, it was seldom that a
member of any class outside and above the Working
Class took the trouble to turn up at our meetings.
They were found to be more likely to instruct the
police to harry us and prevent our meetings.

If I go on in this strain, my talk will sound more
like an indictment of the Working Class than of the
Capitalist Class. Did you, fellow workers, ever come
to the assistance of any speaker or writer or poet who
espoused your cause and stood up for you ? Have you
ever read Shelley's *Oedipus Tyrannus, or Swell-foot the
Tyrant* ? Do you know your Shelley ? Not you. You
would have joined the folk who persecuted him, and
tried to make life bitter for him. Did you ever hear
of Ruskin or Edward Carpenter ? Good job for these
that they were well-to-do. Who was it that assisted
Francis Adams, the author of *Songs of the Army of the
Night* when he was in ill-health and poverty-stricken ?
You are the Army of the Night, Oh, Workers. Did

you assist Adams ? A middle-class man, J. W. Barrs, of Leicester, assisted him, and also assisted Evilyn Douglas and James Thomson (B.V.). If Barrs never did anything good in all his life but to harbour and finance and befriend these three, he deserves to be remembered and honoured. Who supplied the sinews of war for the Socialist Propaganda of the nineties ? Middle-class men again like Hyndman and Morris. Who did the glorious statistical spade work ! The Webbs, middle-class people. How did Shaw win through to wealth and popularity ? His Plays were unmitigated attacks on the upper classes and all their works and pomps. Teste *Widowers' Houses* and *Major Barbara*. His satire drew patronage from the very class he was satirising. It was new to them to be attacked and laughed at, and they shelved and put aside the attacks and the thoughts they contained for the sake of the laughter. They were tickled. You workers never patronized him, so the Bourgeois treated the attacks as a joke. "He's down on us" they said "and no mistake ; but let's pretend we think he's only joking : the masses don't understand him anyhow : so *we* are safe ; where's the danger? Go on G.B.S., give us some more." My sister Kate was explaining to a girl-shopmate how under Socialism we workers could work fewer hours for more money, and be better dressed and housed and fed, and need never die poor. "Oh, Ild' go in for that," said the girl, "When is it coming off ? " That question requires answering. We may be dreaming about something that could "come off," and would if we wanted it. No bloody revolution would be safe in bringing it about, because violence does not convince ; and 'tis hard to think of bringing heterogeneous masses to the point and pitch of any kind of revolution. If the number required to make a successful revolution were obtainable, change could be accomplished without firing a shot. Will it be an upheaval or will it be gradual ? Will it take place at all or is it only a beautiful dream ? Is it right to insist so much on a division of society into classes, seeing that often a working-man is found with all the spirit and inclination of the exploiting middle and upper classes—wanting nothing but means, while there are middle and upper class men, in heart and spirit Revolutionists and Socialists, wanting nothing but opportunity ? Archibald Gorrie is such a middle-class man. Whenever the train-fare to bring a speaker from another town was wanting, or the rent for a hall to speak in was deficient, Gorrie's hand went into his purse, and the sum was made up ; for years he was our financial stay and back-bone, and his right hand never knew what his left did. Years after his accession to our movement I remember asking him one evening, "How did you first come into it, Gorrie." "Don't you know ? " he replied, "Well, I'll tell you. I was coming down Humberstone Gate one Sunday, and I saw a man on top of a dray holding forth ; I said to myself 'What would this babbler say ? ' And, behold he was talking Socialism. And after listening awhile I said 'Well, if that's Socialism, I'm a Socialist.' *And you were the speaker*." I felt proud. I believe I may claim Fred Richards the Shoe Trade Organiser, George Banton the ex-M.P., and two ex-Mayors of Leicester, to wit, Jabez Chaplin and Amos Sherriff, among my pupils. Sherriff used to come and listen to us in Russell Square while he still belonged to the Salvation Army. George Kelly, the dentist, who helped largely in the founding of Wesley Hall, was yet another.

I have belonged at different times to the Social Democratic Federation, Socialist League, Anarchist-Communist Group, and the I.L.P., and have always discountenanced one party's unfriendly criticism of another party. We are unanimous as to our object, but disagree as to the best methods of accomplishing it. Is it, however, all nothing but a beautiful dream— this Socialism ? Even if it is but a dream, I'm glad I dreamed it, and I'm not an inch nearer taking the existing reality to heart. Curse the Reality ! And those who accept it I needn't curse, for, unfortunately they are cursed already.

Does anybody in Leicester now remember, I wonder, a Free-lance Journal called *The Countryman* that came out in the year 1886 ? Is there a file in the British Museum ? What do you mean by *Countryman* ? Well, in contradistinction to Townsman, see ? Every villager 's a countryman. J. W. Barrs, a well-to-do and well-known tea merchant, hearing through friends that I had been for a long time short of work at Cooper and Corah's, and recognising perhaps that I had some literary ability, proposed that I should canvas for advertisements as a stepping-stone towards floating a free Paper. Never mind the mixed metaphor of the last sentence. I had met Barrs several times at the Secular Club, and knew him through taking part

in the Society's lectures and discussions. I think it
was a bee that had been buzzing for a long while in
his bonnet, this project of a Free-lance paper with a
free distribution. We all know that advertisements
are the back-bone of your ordinary newspaper, and
that given a sufficient number of these to finance the
cost of printing and distributing, there's no reason
why a paper couldn't be given away. Country people
bought very few papers, but one that could be had
without money and without price,—Ah ha ! It was
thought to be a want in the villages. Barrs's object
was simply to get a journal in which one could express
his thoughts and feelings, however unconventional,
without let or hinderance, and he guaranteed me
one pound a week for six months, sink or swim. On
this more than hint I took the thing on, and we
swam. Five thousand were given away monthly, and
I got the "ads" and procured distributing agencies in
fifty different Leicestershire villages. I also collected
accounts, read printer's proofs, supplied "copy,"
etcetera.

On leaving the factory my appetite increased
forthwith, owing to my breathing better air ; *crede
experto*. But——, Rejoice all ye tens of thousands in
factory and workshop ; again I say Rejoice ! Ye do
something ; ye create something : ye saw and weld
and plane and hammer, and accomplish something.
Glorious, if ye had but more and better air to breathe !
Yes, I know about the stink of the dye-vat and I
deplore the pestilent unwholesome mine. These are
vile, but not so damned demoralising as soliciting for
orders or "ads." How do you feel after you have

called on half-a-dozen Tradesmen, and two were
almost contemptuous, and two were irritable, and
two were too busy, so that you have to retire till
next day ? Don't you feel that you want to call in at
the nearest hostelry and have a drink ? Don't you ?
Well, I'm sorry to say I *did*, though I willingly admit
this also was demoralising.

How the villagers must have blinked and stared !
We didn't consider whether we were giving them
what they wanted : we gave them what we thought
they ought to want. All the Clubs and Coffee-houses
in Leicester that were agreeable to accept a copy
were supplied. We were Socialists and Secularists,
and criticised mercilessly the conventions—theological,
political and industrial. It may be that our out-
spokenness gained readers, but advertisers often
fought shy of patronising such a paper. We invited
correspondence on any and every subject and promised
to print it just as it reached us ; no curtailment, no
alteration. If correspondence was not forthcoming,
well, I invented it, and then replied to myself in the
next issue very effectively : who is it that couldn't
knock down his own man of straw ? There was
another free paper—*The Village Advertiser*, smaller in
size, pious in tone ; and the editor and proprietor,
canvassing for "ads," saw fit to speak ill of our paper
and run it down on the score of propriety and
morality. Oh, we were a bad lot, and no mistake.
This I learnt from different shop-keepers as I went
my rounds. Now the same *Village Advertiser* ran a
Phrenological business, delineating character by photo,
and making a charge for the delineations. I told

Barrs how his paper was being abused, and I showed a copy of the *Advertiser*. "Well, look here," said he, "we'll just turn the tables on this joker. He makes a charge for his delineations ; why can't *we* delineate by photo ? And we'll only charge a penny stamp for the return of the photo. I'll help you." He said he would, but the beggar never did. I cannot say though that I found the added duty of delineating a burthen : I was so interested. My work was pure guess-work, but whatever may be thought or said, I was often remarkably right on the admission of the people delineated. You see, you needn't mention faults or badness. What Phrenologist is there who says to a subject "you are rather mean—and selfish—envious—careless of other's rights—vain and boastful and given to deceit and lying" ? Oh no ! We never mention it. "Professor Blague" was my *nom de plume* for this job, and here is a specimen of the delineations—

"Ivy.—This young lady has a slight build, but is lithe and supple of limb, and of splendid physical proportions. One great difficulty of the physiognomist, if he happens to be impressionable, is, that in describing a handsome girl, he is liable to have his mental powers distracted by the mysterious influence of the beauty of his subject—to become mesmerised, as it were, when the mind needs to become concentrated on her mental and moral qualities. Ivy's insanitary fashion of wearing the hair as a fringe descending upon the forehead, has placed us under the necessity of calling in the aid of Hypnotism. We had to throw a friend into a sort of trance in order

that he might see the top of the forehead. The
result of the clairvoyant diagnosis is quite in accord-
ance with our anticipations. Ivy is sharp, quick-
witted, intelligent. Very practical. Not given to
moon and mope. Not cast down by misfortune.
Considerably imaginative ; but checking the imagination with good sense. Not superstitious ; giving little
credit to dreams and fortune-telling. Confident and
self-reliant. Will influence her husband by her will-
power. Has a great capacity for enjoyment, and is
excessively fond of the good opinion of others. All
the moral faculties well developed." (Photo returned.)

How long this Character Reading lasted I don't
now remember, but *The Countryman* itself lasted about
six years. When advertisers failed to pay, Barrs
never prosecuted, never took out a summons. The
paper had never, I think, made a profit, and ultimately
the falling off in revenue from advertisements com-
pelled Barrs to cease publication. My experience
with this paper convinced me that any position
involving such responsibility as attaches to present-
day business was utterly foreign to my poor idiosyncrasy. I declare that years after having done with
The Countryman, I used to wake up with nightmare,
worrying about printers and "ads", full of anxiety
and fear of being behind-hand with the next issue
of the paper.

Though I knew J. W. Barrs about a quarter of a
century, it was all on one side,—the literary and
artistic side. I have previously referred to him as the
friend and patron of neglected writers and men of
genius—Barlas, author of *Phantasmagoria*, Francis

Adams, author of *Songs of the Army of the Night*, and
James Thomson (B.V.), author of *The City of Dreadful
Night*. To Thomson, in great part, Barrs owed the
formation of his literary tastes and predilections.
'Twas a habit with him to purchase and read any book
that the popular and ordinary critics condemned ;
the heavier the condemnation, the better he expected
the book to be. You could always be sure, he said,
that a book treated like that was well worth reading.
He was all but a total abstainer. I have been to dinner
and supper with him at Chantry House, The Newarke,
scores of times, but there was never any beverage on
the table stronger than claret, and claret not often.
Tobacco, in the form of cigarettes, was his weakness ;
he knew the frequent cigarette was injuring his eyes,
and I've heard him regret that his efforts to renounce,
or restrict it, were futile : *au contraire*, I eschewed
cigarettes, but had the ordinary Irish penchant for a
drop of whisky. He was a lover of pictures, and was
specially fond of George Morland's, while I could
never muster any great admiration for George ;
there seemed to me a sameness in the painter's apple-
cheeked slatternly figures, shaggy ponies, and scraggy
sharp-snouted pigs. The Chantry House book-
shelves contained volumes by writers I had never
heard of before, such as Marcus Clark, Garth
Wilkinson, and Herman Melville ; and flanking and
overlying these were our old friends Rabelais, Mon-
taigne, Boccaccio, Borrow, Balzac, Hugo, Zola,
Meredith, George Moore, Thomas Hardy, Tolstoy,
Whitman, Leopardi, Villon and *mony mair* !

CHAPTER V

RUSKIN, MORRIS, CARPENTER, SHAW

IF you met a working man—merely a proletarian working man too—who had once received a letter from Ruskin, had visited Edward Carpenter, dined and chatted with William Morris, and walked a mile or two along with Bernard Shaw, wouldn't you say the man hadn't lived in vain, and ought to feel proud ? Well, such a man am I ! A letter from Ruskin ? you exclaim. Yes. While I was managing *The Countryman*, previously referred to, I made a kind of abridgment of *Unto This Last*, and got a local printer to print off a number of copies. It was in pamphlet form and sold at a penny. I never made a penny by it, and didn't want ; my object was propaganda purely. The title of the pamphlet was *The Rights of Labour according to John Ruskin*, then, in smaller type, "Arranged by Thomas Barclay." A friend meeting me some days after publication asked me whether I had had Mr. Ruskin's permission. Well, I hadn't : I never thought about it. In some trepidation I sent a copy to him, as well as a letter explaining, offering at once to stop further publication if he demanded it. Instead of demanding suppression of publication, here is an extract from the letter he sent me. "Your pamphlet is the best abstract of all the most important pieces of my teaching that has yet been done ; and I am entirely grateful to you for doing it, and glad to have your letter." The full letter is in the keeping of the Liverpool Ruskin Society.* I had no means of publishing on any large scale, and gave the socialist publisher, W. Reeves of Fleet Street, London, full leave to publish the pamphlet. It reached several editions.

About 1890 I was Leicester delegate to a Conference of the Socialist League held in a room in Farringdon Street, London ; Belfort Bax, Frank Kits, and Halliday Sparling were of the company. After business we had a little lunch, and I had the honour and pleasure of sitting next to William Morris. I had just been reading William Blake, the Rougon-Macquart Novels, and two or three by George Meredith. I put questions. Yes, Morris liked Blake, "all that any mortal can understand of him." I don't think he'd read many of Zola's novels, but *Germinal* was among the number, and was thought to be really great. Then I mentioned Meredith.   Morris's voice grew suddenly raspy ; Meredith's style he couldn't have at all. "Meredith ! " He dug fist into palm vehemently "Meredith ! He tweaks you by the nose ; he makes me feel I'd like to punch his head ! " Nice thing for one great man to say of another, eh ? Never mind William. You also said Meredith reminded you of a school-boy. We know what you meant, of course : the school-boy often uses long-tailed words, and circumlocutions,

*Enquiry has elicited the fact that the Liverpool Ruskin Society is no longer in existence—it became defunct twenty or thirty years ago. Persistent efforts to trace the actual letter have failed. The Library Edition of Ruskin's Works, Vol. 17, page 9, contains a reference to Mr. Barclay's pamphlet "The Rights of Labour According to John Ruskin," and a *portion* of Ruskin's letter to Mr. Barclay including the passage quoted opposite, but not the whole letter. [This information was supplied to me by the Curator of the Ruskin Museum at Sheffield, to whom I tender my thanks.—*Editor.*]

thinking it's grand so to do. But William, I'm sure you would acknowledge that *The Egoist, Diana of the Cross-ways,* and *The Ordeal of Richard Feverel,* are, apart from style, good food for the intellectual. I wish I had asked you your opinion of Thomas Hardy, and—Ah—How about Browning ? Would you have parodied *The Ring and the Book* as Calverley did in *The Cock and the Bull* ? Ah well ; I wish myself George that you would say "He shook his head" instead of "His head performed the negative." But, I like you both : I like *The Glittering Plain* and *News from Nowhere* immensely : but I also like *One of Our Conquerors* in spite of a couple of pages or so being taken up with describing the event of a man tripping and falling down over a strip of orange-peel.

Now for Edward Carpenter. The author of *Towards Democracy,* like the author of *The Earthly Paradise,* has no "side" or "starch" about him. I heard him say that he called at the village ale-house now and then of a night and sat with the company, and I'm quite sure it was not for want of a drink, but simply from a spirit of camaraderie. I and my friend Gorrie visited him at his home at Millthorpe in Derbyshire, a few miles this side of Sheffield. We were in the garden and Gorrie wanted to photograph Edward : I, being close to him at the time, sidled away that he might be photographed alone ; but no, he made me sit down beside him, and we were taken together : my friend James Kelly has a copy of the photo, and that's more than I have. At tea, I couldn't help but remark how bright and clean and orderly everything was—floors and furniture and crockery and all : then George Merrall, Edward's housekeeper, made us laugh. He told us that being one day in an upstairs room with the window open he heard two women talking to one another as they came along the lane underneath. "There isn't a woman about the place, I tell you" said one. "But who's polished this, and who's scrubbed the other, and who's cleaned all those." "I popped my head out of the window," said Merrall, "and replied 'I did madam.'" The woman looked up, and, going back a pace or two, said "Then I wish you were *my* husband."

Do I presume to write about Bernard Shaw ? Yes, I do, and feel no little pride that I was able to appreciate him very long before some other readers noticed anything remarkable about him. Yes ; after G. K. Chesterton, after Joseph McCabe, after Professor Henderson, after Mons. Hamon, Miss Deacon, Herbert Skimpole and J. S. Collis have written about him, I wish to say something. Who is Miss Deacon, I wonder ; I hope she's alive and well ; her little book was about the first appreciation of Shaw to appear, and I sincerely honour her for it. I have four or five pals, living or departed, who love some author specially ; and I call them by the name of the author :

Charley Crisp is Thomas Hardy.

Fred Hollis is John M. Robertson.

Jack Jennett is H. G. Wells.

George Kelly (God rest his soul ! as the Irish say) is Samuel (Erewhon) Butler.

And I, Tom Barclay, am Bernard Shaw.

I've often wondered whether there are proletarian worshippers like me in other towns—Nottingham,

Birmingham, Leeds, Manchester, Glasgow, etcetera ;
there ought to be, though I've never heard of them.
It's high time a Bernard Shaw Society was founded,
but I'm too old and far gone now to agitate for it.
Bernard is generally lucid as well as forceful, but
there are things a Society might explain, as for instance why every man over forty is a scoundrel, and
why music is the brandy of the damned. I met him
years ago while I was living in London, and after
a good long walk and talk he invited me to pay him
a visit ; I haven't paid it yet, but——well I'm somewhat
diffident now : I've nothing to say more than I've
said to him in letters, and a great literary man, I'm
afraid, is often pestered with callers until he hardly
has a quiet hour to call his own. Well, as I said I'm
a worshipper ; but I'm as inconsistent as the Christians
who worship Christ and do not follow his example.

I think a letter I wrote to G.B.S. some years ago is
worth inserting here.

July 21st, 1908.

DEAR SHAW,—I'm the chap that met you, some six
years ago now, where Oxford Street cuts Soho Street
or Soho Square ; you remembered me as coming
from Leicester, and being acquainted with James
Billson, and having been connected with—I think
you remembered that—a paper called *The Countryman*.
It was several years before that since you had met
me, and that only once or twice, so I was surprised at
your prodigious memory and highly gratified when
you explained that you generally remembered anyone
that had anything remarkable about him. Like the
Walrus and the Carpenter we walked on a mile or so

and talked of many things ; I said I should like to visit you and be introduced to the good lady your wife (absent-minded that I am, I never thought of asking after your mother) ; you said "Come whenever you like." I had to leave London soon after that but I haven't forgotten ; I mean to pay that visit some day ; surely if people go to America to see Whitman, and to Russia to see Tolstoi I shall go as far as London to see Shaw. I met James Billson a couple of years ago ; he had recently been in London and had talked with you. I asked for personal details of you—mentally personal details let me say—for I despise the babble of externals and accidentals we get in the smart Reviews. I felt the natural interest we all feel in a genius, and you are one who uses it (genius) for the good of others. That's it ; I like you and admire you for other and better qualities than genius, and if other proletaires do not everywhere like you as well it is because the poor beggars do not know you or are too stupid.

Probably you feel you do not deserve this, but I must express what I feel and hope you'll take an honest pleasure in being praised as Ruskin used. We see laudation lavished on men for nothing and for worse than nothing—for positive injury—and shall we be ashamed of speaking a word of love and sympathy to a really worthy man until he is dust and ashes and cannot know that our heart and mind ever stirred in kindly intelligent response to his ? Well, I wanted to get your attitude towards things, and Billson tells me you are keenly alive to every move in the Social game. I might have known it—something

like your own Trefusis or Jack Tanner. You see, I'm
supposed not to be a level-headed judge of you.
Friends in Leicester say I've got Shaw on the brain ;
I wish *they* had Shaw on the brain, or better still, *in*
the brain. They tell me what you say in *Man and
Superman* is not new ; I tell them that you say so
yourself. They say that you are a vogue that will
pass ; you say that too in one of your prefaces. *"Tout
passe, tout casse."* How does that prove anything
against you ? You're pessimistic too it seems. There
is cause enough, goodness knows, but whatever
else you are, *that* you are not, but a hearty and
heartening optimist, not of the can't-see-anything-
amiss kind, but hoping while there is hope : optimistic
philosopher and lover of philosophers, *vide* your
eulogy of them in *Man and Superman.* In all I have
ever read of your writings I fail to find any maundering
or moaning or groaning ; yet you deal with the very
subject-matter that makes mad the pessimist—slums
and prostitution and wholesale murder, sudden and
slow. The Life-force worshipper a Pessimist, Pooh !
The way these chaps talk you might have been out-
pouring like a Thomas Hardy or a "B.V." You are
an optimist too on such meagre pabulum, in such a
strange way, at such a disadvantage : many of us
men and sub-men *would* be pessimists but that we
find surcease of sorrow in drugging ourselves with the
things of the senses, whereas you will not touch
tobacco, nor drink fire-water, not eat "corpse," nor
frequent race-meets, nor sully yourself with Mrs.
Warren's Profession. And you do not feel you're
doing penance in abstaining from these, you simply

abhor them. I read too that you do not even drink tea. I wish you were not quite like this ; it makes *nous autres* afraid of you : you might assume a vice if you have it not. I was going to say you might attend the play, but you are human enough on the play-acting side ; it must, though, take a deuce of a play to entertain the author of *Widowers' Houses* and *Arms and the Man*. When I come to think of it how could it be otherwise ? I believe you would be ashamed of writing a play merely for pastime and to amuse us. Your play is but the form of your message, and the fun is but a kind of condiment that renders the message palatable. When are your productions going to be staged here ? In a big town like Leicester the best we have ever seen are *Leah Kleshna*, *Walls of Jericho*, and *His House in Order* : even these are like angels visits. There is every chance for the mad mechanic melodrama and the vacuous Variety Hall rubbish, but no chance of seeing a play of yours. Incidentally, what a comical forecast of the theatre of the future was that you did for one of the smart magazines. I am not surprised my friends don't understand you sometimes ; I'm afraid you give ordinary people a totally wrong impression of your meaning by your hyperbolism and over-emphasis, and thus defeat your object ; for we cannot do without the ordinary people, it seems to me, the rest of us are so few. You often seem to myself "a bundle of contradictions." The man who, while having to trim his coat-cuffs with a pair of scissors, announces himself as an exploiter of labour living out of others to the best of his ability, is an enigma : you remember

Mrs. Besant denouncing you as a loafer and afterwards apologising ; did you invite that denunciation
on the score that a press-man is no true producer ?
I have watched your career for a long time you see,
yet I seem to be no better for your teaching and
example.   I am like the christians who believe in
Christ but will not imitate him.   Yes, I have watched
you right from the time when some of "The Seven
Against Society" as J. M. Robertson called ye, ye
used to exercise with the gloves, and when G. W.
Foote, observing that you turned up at every progressive meeting extant, called you "ubiquitous G. B.
Shaw."   I read you in *The Christian Socialist* before
Justice existed, and even then (and you must have been
a very young man) you had all the insight and wit and
irony and charm that distinguish you from every
living English (I must not say Irish) writer that I
know of except, and these are lesser stars, H. G.
Wells (*The Wonderful Visit*), Richard Whiteing,
Israel Zangwill, and Cunningham Graham.   These,
though, haven't your breadth and depth.   You might
say of me here "This fellow tells me what I know
very well and what is known to everybody."   Unfortunately this is not so ; there are thousands and
millions who never heard of you.   I am not un-
gratefully unmindful of other reformers and revolutionists inside and outside the Fabrian Society, but
you alone seem to possess that divine gift, an expression
that can arrest the cultured and capable among us.
I may tell you though that in my opinion G.B.S.
might be as witty and brilliant as he liked and my
class would have found little permanent enjoyment

in him : it is G.B.S., the Socialist and Revolutionist, that claims our affectionate allegiance. I exult that in spite of our density and apathy he has never been tempted to throw us over. You have forced your way to the top in spite of unconventionalism being such an unmarketable commodity : *Deo gratias* ! I thank you from the bottom of my heart and with all the grey matter of my cerebrum for many a delightful hour passed spell-bound in the absorption of your hilarious wisdom. My reason for saying that you are not an Irish writer is of course a Gaelic League one. I see in the preface to *John Bull's Other Island* criticism of the Gaelic League which, an I understand it aright, I do not agree with, but never mind ; of that another time. I must have a talk with you about J.B's other Island ; I trembled while that Glasgow-Irishman was on the stage in the first scene, wondering could you have bungled the brogue, and when I found that you hadn't I chortled in my joy, and so did my sister who has read your things nearly as avidly as myself. You are a good Irishman anyhow, though William Archer, confound him, wants to make you out no Irishman at all but a Scandinavian, on the mere strength of your name. I took this particularly hard as we Irish have had so few philosophers. I'm glad to see you contributing to the Seancicuid ; I've never seen it myself but I see by the writers what it must be like : "Pat" in the *Saturday Review* is a little like you. I have read Voltaire and Moliere and Heine and Aristophanes (*Plutus* is your only comedy for us moderns) and I find that finer than any of these is Bernard Shaw. I'm laughed at for saying that *Man and Superman* is better than *Faust*, but I say it again : it is the greatest play was ever written. The philosophy too is condensed and up-to-date, a god-send to the intellectual proletaire, who after sixty hours a week in shop or shed, hasn't time and energy for the exhaustive and exhausting tome philosophic ; *Man and Superman* boils down and gives us to drink of the essence of Philosophy. It is your special glory that as dramatist the Revolutionists' and Reformers' object has always been kept first with you, and that literature and other considerations have had to take their chance. How I rejoice that in the face of all that has been against you, you have come into your own while still alive—rather that we through you have come into our own, or part of our own. Grant Allen says in *Philistia* something to this effect, that the Aristocrat has his past to look back upon and the working man his future to look forward to, while the middle-class man has nothing but his money ; don't think I'm too class-conscious, but you'll know what I mean : you might have made money by merely amusing the privileged classes at our expense, and instead of that you have pitched into them unafraid and fought tough battle after battle for poor devils like me, it may be while I was frivolling or getting drunk after the manner of my class. I should like to be a believer for a minute just to be able to say "God bless you" ! I remember how when Sir Walter Besant presumed to amend Ibsen by writing a continuation of Nora's career after leaving the Doll's House, you took up the cudgels for the Master, answering Besant with what *you* thought the true version of what happened to Nora :—how you dealt too with W. H. Mallock's *Trumpet-call* in the *Fortnightly*. *Herr Gott* ! What smithereens you did make of him. I read in *Time* your little non-age story *The Miraculous Revenge*, which if my memory serves me had no more purpose than a Kipling story : of course you had not found yourself, and I merely mention it to show how far back I began to take an interest in you. "Hello ! " I said ("What-ho" hadn't then come up) as I lit upon *An Unsocial Socialist* in *To-Day*, which you said ought to be *To-Morrow*, "Here's a new one, a genius" ; and since then I have read everything of yours I could lay my hands on, especially if I didn't have to pay for it. And now I'm told that a certain Professor Henderson has come all the way from America to write your biography. I envy him the distinction ; what has he done to merit it ? I ought to have discovered you and written that biography, but I was always a day after the fair. *The Clarion* has done you a good turn at times, but its reviews of *Man and Superman* and *The Doctor's Dilemma* seemed worded to prejudice the public against you ; the impression people would get of the plays is that they are outrageously improbable. One would expect better from the unconventional *Clarion*. re *The Doctor's Dilemma*, I read paper after paper— *Morning Leader*, *Daily Chronicle*, *Stage*, *Era*, etcetera, and laughed at the point-blank way they contradicted one another. I read that article in *Blackwood* by the anonymous one, and it's clear he's not only in Swinburnian phrase "cankerous with malevolence" but hopeless with hypocrisy as well, or he'ld have tackled the writer of the able article on you in the *Edinburgh.*

I wish to conclude this long letter by asking why you say in the *Revolutionists' Handbook* that every man over forty is a scoundrel ? Of course I'm making you responsible for *Jack Tanner.* Anyhow, the saying's as enigmatical as the fact that every blessed photo of you differs from every other. In *The English Illustrated* you look like a mild Buddha ; in *The Academy* you've a sardonic smile ; in Frank Harris's *Candid Friend* you scowl ; in *The Bystander* you appear to be in torment ; and in others you are not yourself at all.

Good-bye now, and give my kind regards to your wife—and to your mother if she is, as I trust she is, still in the land of the living.

Yours truly,

THOMAS BARCLAY.

All that is best in me is alive and alert whenever Shaw is mentioned : if anyone praises Shaw I feel ready to hug him : if anyone attacks Shaw I take him on in argument, and then I find that the attacker either hasn't read Shaw at all, or cannot understand him, or he's like the Devil in *Man and Superman.* Shaw seems to me to have the deepest thought and the clearest expression of it about everything that's worth studying. So why bother about anyone else ?

CHAPTER VI

THE GAELIC LEAGUE AND IRELAND

ONE day, somewhere in the nineties, I became impressed (I might say *obsessed*) with the thought that I couldn't be really Irish without a knowledge of the Irish language. I'm doubtful now in this year of 1925 whether this is correct : it seems to me that men like Wolf Tone, Robert Emmett, John Mitchell, Philpot Curran and Henry Grattan are enough to confound anyone who holds that the old tongue must be used before one can call himself Irish. Be that as it may, I started on the old language for all I was worth, and that which immediately influenced me was the series of simple lessons by Father O'Growney that ran daily in the Dublin paper, *The Freeman's Journal*. I had been three or four years earning a living by distributing from house to house Tradesmen's leaflet advertisements : the pay was two shillings and sixpence a day, and rainy days I had to stand by. I got a similar job in London for a Jewish firm of artificial teeth-makers. My circuit was Paddington, and from thence, my day's work being done, I took a 'bus to wherever the Gaelic League held its classes—Bedford Street, Strand, or Athenæum Hall, Tottenham Court Road, or Chancery Lane. During the eighteen months I lived in London, I think I never missed a single lesson.

How does it strike you great thinkers and movers of the world—statesmen, philosophers and such ?

Here was a bunch of people, some fifty all told, bent
on reviving Irish as a spoken tongue (see prospectus
of Gaelic League), in the very heart of the most
indifferent, if not the most inimical, city in the world :
they got no help even from the rest of their fellow-
countrymen residing in London.   But it didn't
matter. One point of view will regard them as Quixotes
tilting at windmills, but another point of view will
regard them as exiled patriots, clinging to the music
and manners and language and lore of their fore-
fathers.   Besides, if philological savants like Zeuss,
Windisch, De Joubainville, and Kuno Meyer——Oh,
but I'm forgetting ; they are perhaps only interested
in "Celtic"—if these, I was going to say, could be
interested in Gaelic, how then should not the
immediate descendants of the Gaels themselves ?

Allow me to say here that I'm not writing a history
of the League for the space of the year and a half
that I lived in London, but just giving my impressions.
I don't remember ever seeing a priest at any of the
meetings or classes, but perhaps there were no Irish
priests in London. How things are now I do not
know, except that classes are much more numerous.
What a set of enthusiasts we were, most of us from
County Kerry, Munster, and employed in the Customs, or the Post Office. I don't remember that there
was a single member from Manchester or Liverpool
or the Potteries ; but what of that ? The Irish in
those places had, no doubt, their own branches of
the Gaelic League, and were under no necessity of
migrating to London. I was from Leicester, and
Leicester's "different."

A fact worth noting is that men who attended the same classes with me, like Pierce Beasley and W. P. Ryan, can now write plays and novels and give addresses in Irish. Pupils had some chance of getting acquainted with all the three principal dialects ; P. T. Macginly was an Ulsterman, and Michael Brennan was brought over specially from Connemara. Other teachers were Fionan MacColm, Sean O'Cahan and Dr. Henry. Dr. Henry is now professor of Irish in Galway University : he was a genial Connaught man, and his knowledge of grammar was great. I don't know how he obtained his knowledge, but he appeared to know every twist and turn of the modern language : I think he must have read all the grammars that preceded his *Handbook of Modern Irish*, and must have consulted Irish speakers from all parts. But 'twas not grammar and variety of phrase that alone we needed ; 'twas more spoken lessons and more frequent intercourse. I remember rising and asking at a meeting whether it wasn't possible to have classes nightly instead of the hour and a half weekly that we were having : I contended that the sounds of the old tongue died out of our memory during the hundred and odd waking hours of the week. My question and contention raised a considerable discussion, but the end of it was, if I remember rightly, that we hadn't the means of meeting the expense of nightly classes. We didn't know much of one another I think ; I question if a single member knew anything about me, save that I was from the Midlands. But this was not to be wondered at : outside the classes what chance had we ? We came from various parts of London, and soon as arrived at class-room business commenced. Business over, we must fly East, West, North and South by 'bus and tube. On certain nights though we had a dance for half an hour after lessons—jigs, single and double, and four-handed reels, and I remember that a number of young men turned up for the dance, but avoided the lessons : soon after noticing this we put our foot down : we declared we were only incidentally a dancing academy, and insisted on "No lesson, no dance." I remember dimly a Miss Agnes Machale and a Miss (now Dr.) Annie Peterson or Patterson. These ladies used to play for us at all our dances and concerts. I remember, also rather dimly, a dancing master named Reidy, and a professional dancer, Jack O'Brien. A lady I remember specially and very clearly was a Miss Edith Drury, now Mrs. Costelloe, wife of a Tuam M.D. She was an enthusiast for Irish Folk Music, and since going back to live in Ireland has collected and published, under the auspices of the Irish Folk-song Society, Songs of Galway and Mayo, the most delightful Irish chanties and melodies I have ever come across : other West of Ireland collections there may be quite as meritorious, but I have not seen or heard them. Mrs. Costelloe gives a translation of the words of every melody.

Sean O'Cahan was a serious teacher, but not too serious to do a step or two in a dance : W. P. Ryan wrote of him that probably no one ever knew him when he wasn't working in some way or other on behalf of the Old Tongue : he introduced us to the Berlitz system of teaching. Macginly favoured the

Photograph of G.B.S. given to Barclay by Shaw
(Note "Tom Barclay" written on the photograph by Shaw)

Francis A. Fahy

During his time in London, with the Gaelic League, Barclay was
influenced by the enthusiasm and hard work of men such as Francis
Fahy, who was the organiser and guiding spirit of the Southwark Junior
Irish Literary Club in the 1890s. Another of Barclay's acquaintances in
this cultural milieu, William Patrick Ryan, described Fahy's initiatives as
being "suggestive of a Government Department in their minuteness and
complexity, and illustrate quite a system of Irish national education"
(Ryan, W.P. (1894), *The Irish Literary Revival*, p.14)

Gouin system, and published a book of lessons on that system for the use of teachers : he was an arduous and untiring worker.   MacColm was well liked by his scholars, but he limited himself to the Munster dialect.   What was Patrick O'Connor doing among us, I wonder ? I really can't recollect, but he was not learning Irish : he had his budget full of it already —full to the extent of being able to write dramatic and realistic novels in the tongue.   Art O'Brien and Francis Fahey were also among us—in the capacity of officials, I believe.

On August 1st, 1901, a dozen or so of us met for a literary evening at 8 Adelphi Terrace, and I contributed an effusion in Irish—a kind of game similar to *The House that Jack Built*, entitled "Let the short hen go round." A group sat in a circle, so my mother said, from whom I had learned the game, and the hen was passed imaginatively from neighbour to neighbour right round. She is questioned as to her brood, and the brood grows from one starling, two white doves, and so on as she passes, to monstrously Brobdignagian bulks and multitudes. Professor Ahern of Waterford denied vehemently that my mother could have used a particular word meaning "short" in the sense of "little," but I had to assure him that she really did.   But there was too much bending over books I tell you to learn to speak ; whether we could help it or not, or whether we understood it or not, we were treating the old tongue a good deal as though it were a dead language. Then too, some of us defaulted at times—spasmodic, erratic, and we listened patiently, W. P. Ryan, to your words upbraiding us for our want of perseverance ; you were puzzled as to whether it was a defect in the national character, I believe : we listened to you with sad smiles at one another : I think we felt that what you were saying couldn't be denied, and we resolved that things shouldn't be so in future. As time went on I became more and more doubtful whether success could be secured by the methods we were employing. We're awake every day of the week sixteen hours or so ; that is as I reckon it one hundred and twelve hours every week : and out of that we were spending one hour, or two hours at the most with Irish—one hundred and ten hours with English that we well understood, and two hours with Irish that we did not understand. Moreover, during the summer months the classes were not running, and the students only met a few times in the open places like Epping Forest. I felt that restricted to such methods I'ld never be an Irish speaker till the day after the "General Resurrection" !

That strenuous MacGinley learned Irish from his mother's lips while still a child ; but—how has W. P. Ryan managed to become so proficient ? I envy the extent and quality of his Irish. I liked Ryan : I think he was the most tolerant, broad-minded and scholarly of all the Irishmen I met in London. I'm just about half-way through a novel of his in Irish, dealing with the mystical and psychical. I've seen nothing else like it in Irish, in spite of the people being so pious. Like MacColm, O'Cahan, Mac-ginly, and O'Connor, Ryan returned to Ireland. *The Irish Nation* that he edited was my ideal of a paper

—patriotic, searching, progressive : but he said something that displeased Cardinal Logue, and— now let me be careful—I haven't the actual facts, and I have no right to set down anything definitely without them. I've got a notion that the Cardinal denounced the paper, but I'm not sure. Anyhow, the paper "went down," *id est*, it ceased publication ; and Ryan returned to London. I had the pleasure of writing a couple of articles for the *Irish Nation* : one was on Dialects, "What to do with the Dialects," and the other recounted my experiences during a visit to Castlebar and district. I had occasion to write a letter on a subject that greatly interested and puzzled me. In *The Irish Nation* ran a serial in the form of fiction, and in this there were discussions on philosophical and sociological subjects : 'twas the first time I had ever seen such things treated of in Irish : the very terminology I had never seen before in that language. There was a nom de plume to the tale—if tale I may call it : I thought Ryan was the author, but in a courteous and complimentary answer to my letter he disclaimed authorship, and was not at liberty to disclose the author's name. I would have been proud to have written that tale.

About 1902 I had to leave my job, through no fault of my own, and return to Leicester, and shortly after I did Macginly visited our town, and brought with him Owen Lochran, a fellow customs officer, working about four miles away at Wigston. We met, a number of us, at St. Patrick's Schools ; a branch of the Gaelic League was formed and I became the teacher. I also taught a class formed at Whitwick,

a small town some twelve miles away where there
are a number of Irish colliers. This class fell through
in less than six months, and the St. Patrick's followed,
gradually dwindling.   Owen Lochran, a north of
Ireland enthusiast, got himself transferred from
Wigston to Castlebar, Mayo, his sole reason being to
perfect himself in Irish among the Connaught
speakers. A young Englishman, Dick Hancock, was
as enthusiastic as any Irishman could possibly be,
and soon caught up to the best of us in speaking ;
when I, becoming disheartened by the laxity and want
of interest, withdrew from teaching, Dick succeeded
me, but eventually the branch died of Anglo-
consumption. But one Irish speaker is left to-day in
Leicester—Maggie Brown : she is the Leicester
equivalent of what Dorothea Pentreath was in
Cornwall ; and I, a would-be Irishman, and Dick
Hancock, an Englishman with a Jewish strain in him,
are the only two who can read an Irish book or
newspaper.

Was it Jonathan Swift that said "Blessed is the
man who is well deceived" ?   I forget, but I wish
sometimes I'm not deceived in regard to Irish ; for
thought and intelligence war on feeling and cry out
"Can't you see that as Manx is following Cornish,
so will Highland Gaelic follow Manx, and Bas-
Breton and Cymric follow Highland Gaelic, and—well,
do you expect a few thousand semi-isolated unlettered
aborigines of Donegal, Connemara, Achill, The
Blaskets, etc., to resist the tide of a language that is
spoken and cultivated by millions and millions in so
many parts of the world ? "

How I regret the criminal and senseless half-tipsiness and general wastefulness of many and many a night, and how must I have been if I had had no liking for books and no ideal whatever to strive for ? Let no one who may happen to see these things I write imagine that I am telling the whole truth and nothing but the truth about myself. I'm omitting to turn my worse side towards you, and why not ? If I stripped my body in a public square I should be arrested and punished, and shall I do something as bad if not worse—strip my poor soul naked before you ? No ; I'm no realist : what would be the good of confessing my short-comings, and mean and selfish actions ? I hate to think about them myself, and why should I create a similar hatred of them in the minds of others ? I prefer to be thought better of : isn't that natural ? But how different I think I *would* be could I have my limited time and limited opportunities over again ! I fear this is mere twaddle though and I may be tempted to strike my pen through it next week. Let's get on with a few adventures.

How did I first get to Ireland ? Some months after the breaking up of the Gaelic classes my friend Owen Lochran wrote me that he was going to the Annual Gaelic Festival, a Festival of piping, singing, dancing, drama and oratory, to be held in Dublin, would I meet him there ? I was working at a Beer-bottling Store for sixteen shillings a week, and my friend knew that most likely I had no money. He sent me five pounds to defray my expenses. He considered himself indebted to me for tuition and maintained it was but payment, but I returned the five pounds with hearty thanks, stating that I was going to save a bit and promising to see him at the next Festival. But next year came and I hadn't saved anything much, and the five pounds arriving again, I accepted this time : the temptation was too great. I met a fellow-student from London on the boat going across, and he informed me that Thomas O'Flannery was on the same boat with us, but I was too shy to get myself introduced. I believe, according to report, that even Dr. MacHenry would acknowledge,—when it came to Old Irish Bardic Lore—that O'Flannery was—but comparisons are odious. Let us thank whatever gods may be for all the scholars. My friend met me at the landing, and we went to the same Hotel together. And next day I was in Tr'na n'Og. I heard at the Rotunda, E. MacNeill and Dr. Douglas Hyde in Irish speeches : I saw the dance competitions : I heard the Irish pipers. We went to Tara where there was a tea followed by a number of speeches, but I don't remember now the names of speakers or anything that was said. When I got a quiet few moments to myself to saunter about, I remember I knelt down and kissed the ground : to me it was holy. I wrote to my favourite sister, Kate, and she replied in a sort of Irish (perhaps my own wasn't perfect) : I'ld have liked to have taken her with me but,—both of us couldn't have gone. Kate, dear loving intelligent Kate, has since passed into the great mysterious eternal.

The second time I visited Ireland I went to a local Gaelic Festival at Castlebar about 1909. Whilst there I tried to find out some tidings of my mother's people who lived in that neighbourhood, but my quest and questions were in vain. How could I expect otherwise after half a century ? I remember how astonished my host, Thomas Cadden, was to find that I could read the New Testament in Irish and yet was baulked in talking Irish after half-a-dozen sentences : the more common-place and simple the sentences, in fact, the more difficult was my expression of them.

The third time I went to the Island of Saints—*and* Sinners, was on this wise. A German who worked at Ellmore's, the Basket-makers of Thurmaston, heard me say in company that I would take any job I could get in Ireland, no matter how ill-paid, as I wanted badly to live in the country. This gentleman came to be foreman on an Osier plantation at Adare, about ten miles from Limerick. The plantation belonged to the Earl of Dunraven, the Devolution man you may have heard of. My German friend wrote me stating that he had an opening for a hand, but that the wages were only twelve shillings a week : I think he was prepared to find me refusing the job, but I accepted. Twelve shillings a week and no half-day holiday on Saturdays ! Can you wonder that the young men employed there were saving up out of their scant wages to get enough money to take them to America ? Adare I found a dead-alive place, and what I had gone for I didn't at all get : I never found a soul that could speak Irish but an old lady, and her daughter laughed mockingly to hear us exchange a few words. My fellow-workers were all Catholics, but as true as I write it, they didn't know what Feast the Church was celebrating on the fifteenth of August :

and I couldn't tell them. We all stopped work that day, but none of us knew what for but that we always ceased from work on that day. I have learnt since that the Feast is some feast of the Blessed Virgin—the Assumption, I think. Peculiar Catholics, eh ? I lodged with that German manager, a kindly disposed fellow who felt sorry that I had made a mistake. 'Twas a strange mixture of dialects in that household : my friend pronounced English like Hans Breitman himself, the wife was a Londoner with a Cockney accent, and the two children spoke with the Brogue they were continually hearing their schoolmates use. After a month or five weeks in this place, I—to use an English idiom—"chucked it," and went to Dublin, but first I stayed a day or two in Limerick. I went about Garry Owen, my father's birth-place, and up and down O'Connell Street ; what a difference between it and Mungret Street ! I saw Sarsfield's statue and—I believe—the Treaty Stone. But I've only a dim notion of Limerick, I didn't see a tenth of it. Arrived in Dublin, I wrote in Irish to the Secretary of the Gaelic League explaining my case, and my motive for being in Ireland. Could he recommend me to anyone for a job, I asked : I was determined to stay in Dublin. I got a reply to my letter containg a note asking a certain manager on the S.W. Railway to set me on. So I started : I forget what the job was called, but I had to clear the rails in the neighbourhood of the station and wheel barrows of rubble about. At the end of a fortnight I hurt my back carrying wet sleepers, and had to leave my job. I felt ashamed of returning to Leicester—beaten and a failure, as it seemed to me, but this, of course, was foolish. My friend Fred Hollis to whom I had lent a little money to enable him to go to a place of work in Glasgow, promptly paid me on my informing him of the strait I was in : not only so but he, unknown to me, wrote to Charles Crisp the Manager of the place I had left at Leicester. He and Crisp were good pals, and the result of the letter was that Crisp wrote to me saying that I might go back to my work at Leicester : so after an interview with Dr. Douglas Hyde, who strongly advised me to go back to my native town, I came back. I had corresponded with Dr. Hyde—"Creeveen" as the Irish so often call him. Soon after seeing his "Love-songs of Connaught" I wrote to him, and sent him a few scraps—Irish sayings I had got from my mother. I don't think there's a man in or out of Ireland that has done more in our day to revive the language than he. But as I said before comparisons are odious. How about Father Peadar O'Leary, and Dr. Sheehan, and Thomas O'Concannon, Fathers O'Growney and Dinneen, Patrick Pierce, and Norma Barthwick ? There's an Irish name for you,—Barthwick ! Have you ever noticed what a number of worthy Irish people have foreign names ? Listen—Tone, Emmett, Mitchell, Tandy, Keating, Butt, Parnell, Yeats, Hopper, Hyde, Sigerson, Russell, Shaw ; and some of these are *ipsior ipsis Hibernis*. You might think Casement was —well, an English name. No : it's a contraction and alteration of MacEsmond, and not a few O's and Macs have been altered similarly. All of which shows that we are a considerable mixture. Your Davises and

Davitts and MacHales may be Celts, but they're
partly Cymric Celts as their names denote, and
Burkes and Powers and Rochfords and Dillons are
indisputably of Norman lineage. The list could be
lengthened : what of Swift, Berkeley, Goldsmith,
Carlton and St. John Ervine ?   Hindeberg, too,
whose name the Irish have Gaelicised to Hennebry ?

I hope and trust that even if the old language dies
out the old tunes will live : I know a good hundred
and fifty of them, jigs, reels, planxties, suantrais,
elegies, and marches. In all the music ever I've heard
what is there that can compare with them ? I feel
more grateful than I can express to men like P. W.
Joyce, Percival Graves, Captain O'Neill, and other
collectors from Bunting down. But what a puzzle
music is—Irish or not— ! Or is it the listener, the
person, that constitutes the puzzle ?   There are
folk-tunes that carry me away, as the saying is : they
fascinate me, while a symphony of Beethoven's only
bewilders me. I'm sorry for this for I *do* admire
Beethoven as a man. Is it some defect in me ? I'm
told I require to hear him five or six times. But why ?
The glorious folk-tunes grip me the very first time.
Who first called them "*folk*-tunes," I wonder ? Oh,
what's in a name ? Verdi, Gounod, Mozart, and
Sullivan are folk, are they not ? What would their
operas be without the tunes ?   Recent composers
are fortunate : we don't know who composed many
of the loveliest airs that were ever composed ; you
and I, my friend, as known authors of them would be
immortalised. There are hundreds of Irish folk-tunes
but Turlock O'Carolan is the only name of an

Irish Composer that I've ever read of. And by the way, where are the Irish hymn-tunes ? The Irish are a very pious people, but I've never heard or read of a single Irish hymn-tune. I said that Music's a puzzle or the listener or *both* : last night at my barber's I heard Herold's *Zampa* broadcast, and was delighted. "Dosen't this beat the tunes ? " I said. On the other hand or in another mood, the "man in the street" seems to me to be a capital judge ; he takes the *Barcarolle* tune and one other out of the *Tales of Hoffman*, and the rest of the composition may then go to Jericho : he's in love with a couple of things from *Poet and Peasant*, but how about the rest of the opera ? Gounod's *Faust* is most likely such a favourite because of the number of solos it contains. Music may be a language—an universal language—but even spoken language can be ungrammatical, slangy, poetical, eloquent or pedantic, all in the same essay or thesis, and this puzzles one. I walked into a music shop and asked for a whistle ; I wasn't explicit enough, but the servitor discovered that what I required was a "bronze keyless flageolet." Mark the dignified difference ! It's a peculiar language, is music. People abused, resisted, condemned Beethoven, and then accepted and idolised him : later, they served Wagner the very same. The critics were just as good musicians before accepting these composers, I suppose, as they were *after* accepting them : strange, isn't it ? You should have heard two shop-mates of mine pitting Handel and Mozart against one another. Handel's "Alleluia Chorus" — nothing like it on earth ! Glorious ! said the one. Pooh ! 'Twasn't in

it with the "Gloria" of Mozart's Twelfth Mass !
the other maintained : I suppose both were right.
Anyhow I'm glad I can enjoy music, though I shouldn't
like to have to define it. It's an Art I suppose—but
what an art ! Just think ! The painter, sculptor and
poet have got their materials—trees, brooks, hills,
dales, clouds, fellow men and women : the architect,
again, copies and uses trees, plains, cliffs and so on.
The music-composer alone starts with nothing outside himself. As I said in an essay I wrote thirty
years ago in a journal called *The Wyvern,* "He is an
absolute creator, for the sounds employed by him
are not a material he works on, but only a medium by
which he conveys his creations to his hearers." I'm
not sure that this thought and the way of expressing
it are not confused and obscure, but this I am sure of,
that music whether lyric or epic is divine when not
trashy, and that if I allow a man to enjoy listening to
fifty or sixty instruments playing together some
sublime composition, he should allow me my humble
but genuine enjoyment of a folk-tune, pathetic or
hilarious, composed by an unknown ancestor of
perhaps hundreds of years ago. And lest we forget,
what has become of the sweet simple Glees, Rounds
and Catches of fifty years ago ? I seldom hear one
except at a Welsh concert : I should be real glad to
see a revival of them.

CHAPTER VII—MORE ABOUT G.B.S.

DOES anyone now read *Ethics of the Dust*, *Sesame and Lilies*, and *The Crown of Wild Olive* ? I'm sure I don't know. Does anyone read Carlyle outside *Sartor Resartus* ? Are Matthew Arnold and Swinburne and Browning superseded ? Tennyson's a back number I fancy, and Thackeray, Lytton, and Dickens are overworn. Does an author now only serve and subserve his own time and generation ? It may be so, and for that reason I'm going to absorb all I can of Bernard Shaw, for I'm only a working man with limited time and means, and the works of Bernard, play-prefaces especially, come the nearest of anything I know to constituting a liberal and up-to-date education.

Never have I known Bernard Shaw to be ruffled or affected by criticism but once, and that was during the Great War. There can be no doubt as to the brutal and malignant character of the criticism of such works as *Common Sense about the War*. One would expect cultured people to be different from the ordinary ones that harried resident Germans, and raided their shops, but no ! Shaw was hurt by the ultra-patriotic newspaper attacks and made a distinct bid for sympathy : he asked that there might be some consideration shown him : he asked, in short, for fair play and justice. 'Twas in vain though that he appealed, for most of us, cultured and uncultured, had lost our heads. Here is an extract from a letter I wrote him at that time. ". . . I can't remain silent in face of your letter to the *Daily Chronicle*. Unfortunately my support of you cannot have public utterance as I am a nonentity ; still I feel I must write to you . . . . What a pity your recommendation of last New Year's day (or twelve months last New Year's day) couldn't have been put into practice ! (I referred to an article in *The Daily News* in which Shaw recommended that our Government should declare plainly that if either Germany attacked France, or France attacked Germany, England would take sides against the aggressor. . . .) If Socialists cannot or will not rally to the call of the deepest and wisest thinker in this country since Morris and Ruskin, then I for one shall begin to think I ought to feel like Thomas Hardy and James Thomson (B.V.)."

Many a time and oft have I wondered how Bernard Shaw—the superman and great humanist—could take such an interest in boxing—in pugilism. Now at last I have discovered the explanation. In *A Note on Modern Prize-fighting*, following *Cashel Byron's Profession* and its dramatisation into *The Admirable Bashville, or Constancy Unrewarded*, Shaw says "The glove fight is a more trying and dangerous form of contest than the old knuckle fight." I understand him to say that the knock-out blow may cause concussion of the brain : but—"The brain as English Society is at present constituted can hardly be considered a vital organ." Never mind the gibe : let's go on and see what Prize-fighting really is. "Exhibition Pugilism is essentially a branch of Art . . . it acts and attracts by propagating feeling . . . sense of danger, dread of danger, impulse to batter and destroy what threatens and opposes, triumphant delight in succeeding : this is pugnacity, the great adversary of the social impulse to live and let live ; to establish our rights by shouldering our share of the social burden ; to face and examine danger instead of striking at it ; to understand everything to the point of pardoning (and righting) everything : to conclude an amnesty with Nature wide enough to include even those we know the worst of : namely, ourselves." He defends the profession only on the same grounds that he defended Mrs. Warren's Profession ; professional boxers are in the same class as "mercenary brides." "Of two things I am certain. First, that glove-fighting is quite as fierce a sport as fist-fighting. Second, that if an application were made to the Borough Council, of which I am a member, to hire the Town Hall for a Boxing Competition, I should vote against the applicants. . . . Put a stop to boxing for money, and pugilism will give Society no further trouble."

Andrew E. Malone states in *Everyman*, August 6th, 1931, "George Moore and Bernard Shaw rarely concern themselves nowadays with Ireland, so they are not spoken about. But their books are all prohibited in Public Libraries. . . . Shaw's plays were condemned to be burned by order of the Public Libraries Committee of the County of Galway, and they cannot be had from the open shelves of an Irish Public Library." Anatole France, H. G. Wells, Conrad, and Galsworthy are also banned. O Lord God!

> "Do I sleep, do I dream, or is visions about ? "
> . . . "Or is the 'Hibernian' played out ? "

I can't help feeling ashamed of the country of my ancestors. Even though some of these writers were proved to be what is called immoral. What *is* immorality in Literature ? I'll leave out the Bible for Catholic reasons, but have the upright, learned, and judicious committees excluded Shakespeare, Swift, Byron, Sterne, Fielding and——Oh give me patience, some divine power ! Do you think, reader, that the committees have really read these authors they've excluded ? "I doubt it" said the Carpenter and shed a bitter tear. If they *have* read them they're not thereby contaminated nor corrupted, of course. They've a greater power of withstanding temptation, these committee-men, than ordinary readers ;—is that it, or what ? Wouldn't it have sufficed them to condemn the authors, or to challenge those alive, like Shaw and Wells, to defend themselves ? Have the rate-payers been consulted, or only the priests ? Won't some Irish youths begin to marvel that Bernard Shaw is banned in Ireland while all the rest of civiliza-tion is reading and applauding him ? These committee-men are, consciously or unconsciously, making the one-time Island of Saints and Sages an Island of Bigots and Omadhauns. It was little likely, I greatly fear me, that Shaw would be read much though there were no ban or interdict, but that leaves the action of the Library Committees none the less pitiable or execrable. Here's an author of thirty-seven dramas, with prefaces,—lengthy, thought-filled prefaces : al-most every play written, not with the object of merely entertaining or amusing, but of teaching, inculcating social truths and duties, exploding noxious errors,

banishing and destroying tyrannies and injustices :
not only this ; not only by means of the drama, but
by lectures, critiques, and essays has he dealt for half
a century with most social evils striving for their
destruction—and we *ban* him. He has been translated
into every language of Europe save two, and we *ban*
him. Seven different men have thought it worth their
while to write Biographies of him,—one of them
coming all the way from an American University,
but *we*, Shaw's countrymen, *ban* him. Well, you see,
we're *Catholics* : we have no right at all to judge for
ourselves on certain subjects. On certain things the
Priests,—Sacred Colleges, Councils, Vatican, have the
right from God to think and decide for the rest of us.
Catholicism *must* regard innovations with mistrust.
There can be no new truths ; no betterment of Society
in the way that certain Saints, and even Popes, have
made out. It is for us, the present living authorities—
canon theologians and such—to interpret or mis-
interpret everything that this or the other writer, lay
or cleric, has said. We can reconcile the most flagrant
contradictions. St. Basil, St. Clement, St. Chrysostom,
and Pope Gregory, the Great, may call the rich man a
"thief" and a "robber"—may argue that "those that
make private property of the gift of God [the land]
pretend in vain to be innocent." What matters it ?
We can put all that right : hear us explain it : we are
perfect and you dare not doubt us : to doubt us
would be sin.

But let me be careful : why is it that Bernard Shaw's
books are excluded from Libraries while his plays are
being played in theatres ? This is a paradox, isn't it ?

I am out of touch with things Irish. What can I do ?
I am poor : I can't afford to send over for a lot of
Anglo-Irish literature ; neither can I visit the country
and investigate : I must though, by some means, get to
know more than I do know. Why not write to the
Gaelic League ? Why, though, bother the League ?
It isn't the Gaelic League's business,—and be careful,
I say again. Don't blame a whole people for what
may be the fault of a few bigots in authority. The
people *en masse* never agitated for a ban on Shaw, Wells
and the others. The great mass may not be bigots at
all, but simply ignorant. I fear there isn't a thoroughly
unbiased Irish newspaper in existence and the *vera
causa* of bans is probably Catholicism. But Russia,
and Italy, and Spain are rebelling against intolerance,
aren't they ? Can Ireland alone withstand the new
spirit, the general trend ? How, I wonder, do Æ and
O'Casey and Yeats and such get on with the priests ?

Catholicism regards almost every new idea, every
step in progress, every discussion of a Social Problem,
with distrust or antagonism. And why ? Well, you
see, Catholicism is perfect and no new truth can be
discovered. Darwinism ? — Monstrous, devilish !
Women's rights ?—Rubbish ! Socialism ?—Wicked,
impossible ! Never mind what certain Saints have
said, or even Popes : we, the present authorities are
the interpreters, and woe unto all who refuse to
acknowledge us.

But leaving Ireland out of discussion, are we in
England here, where no literary production is
banned, more mentally alert and cultured than the
Irish ? I would like to know. We have plenty of

Religions—Four-square Gospellers, Jehovah's Witnesses, Baptists, Mormons, Methodists, Christadelphians, Unitarians, Salvationists, and so on : and as to Sport, we have Greyhound races, Boxers, Footballers, Horse - racing backers, Bookies, Tipsters, Editors, and so on. But very very few of us, religious or non-religious, read or care anything for, Shaw, Wells, Russell, J. M. Robertson, or Upton Sinclair.

I'm very glad Truth is mighty, and is finally going to prevail ; but I wish She'd get a move on. Where does She live ? How does one get acquainted with Her ? Mighty She may be, but so are Her enemies and thwarters — Falsehood, Superstition, Error, Stupidity, Bigotry, Apathy, and Hypocrisy. What have you to say to this, Oh Goddess Truth ? These poor fools can't down Thy servant Bernard Shaw, can they ? Shaw,—novelist, wit, satirist, essayist, dramatist, lecturer, journalist, critic, food and marriage and health and education reformer, social revolutionist, profound thinker and humanist : may the Life-force strengthen you, I pray ! I've just been thinking if a forty-five years reader of you like myself finds difficulty in understanding some of the points of view and contentions in *Back to Methuselah*, how would those points of view and contentions affect the minds of the horse-racing, footballing, beer-swilling, Edgar Wallace reading multitude ? But what use asking ? They'll never read you. They don't know you except by the aborted descriptions of you in the Capitalist newspapers. Don't read any paper that stands up for you, fellow-workers, such as *Forward*, *The Clarion*, *The*

New Leader ; patronize your insidious foes—*The Daily Express, News of the World,* and *Empire News.* You are the class Shaw is specially fighting for : his very first play was written right in the teeth of all that enables a great parasitic moneyed class to own and enslave you and condemn you to the loathsome horrors of slumdom. Have you ever seen the play ? Have you ever read a play of his at all ? I thought you hadn't. And he's the greatest of living play-wrights. Perhaps that's the reason ! Very well— or very ill : if that's how we English, Welsh, and Scottish are, we can't be much better than the Irish. Brailsfords and Ponsonbys and Nevinsons and Morels and Gardiners write for us, but do we read them ? Do we read even Yaffle or Casey or Nun-quam ? What a complex society we are ! While some proletaires are breaking their hearts to try and re-volutionize things for the better, others are boozing, skittling, cinema-seeing, or betraying their class in some way. Vice versa, men like William Morris, Edward Carpenter and Leo Tolstoy are made wretched by watching the filth and squalor of the poor, and use most or all of their mental energies endeavouring to abolish the hellish sufferings that the sufferers them-selves seem to accept and never think of rebelling against.

Is there any record in ancient Greek or Roman history of slave-owners dreaming of or asking for equality of conditions ? I ought to know if I've read Plato's *Republic.* I think I remember that the slaves were often teachers, nurses, household familiars.

I've just finished reading *Back to Methuselah* for

the second time. What a play ! What difficult reading !
I'm puzzled, bewildered : was anything ever written
like it ? A Shaw Society is required were it but to
analyse and criticise this *Metabiological Pentateuch* ; I
suppose Shaw really believes we can live for three
hundred years if we try. Hatched from eggs ; who ?
Why we humans. Eh ? No, he's not paradoxing
or joking. Maturity in four year's time, hardly any
food or clothing or slumber, but sauntering and
soliloquising and contemplating. Read the play.
Never in all my reading have I come across a more
trying, puzzling, fantastic and confounding production. Read it, I say : it conducts us from the
corporeal and carnal to a state in which we are
purely pensive and angelic, and that's a better notion
of things than the idea of Eternal Recurrence.
Recurrence is the twin-brother of Pessimism, and
Shaw is anything but pessimistic. He and Wells are
the only two authors that I know of who project us
several thousand years into the future, and Shaw does
it much more expansively and elaborately than his
Fabian contemporary. Blessings on them both !

Dear Shaw, I must say *As Far as Thought can Reach*
puzzles me. A temple, but no sacrifice nor priest. No
Architecture mentioned. Why set such value on
sculpture ? Is it so much superior to painting ? No
clothing either—or very little. And is it woollen or
purely of vegetable texture ? Who spins and weaves
it, for we have no castes ? Is there any eating, and
where do folk sleep ? Why is sex so persistently
retained, seeing that it is not required for reproduc-
tion ? No other animal is mentioned as far as I

remember. No libraries, nor books nor papers. Oh !
it seems hard ! The ancients are forgetting how to
communicate with the young by language, and what
do the young do with themselves when tired out
dancing to the only kind of music you allude to ?
Gods and games and wars and magical rites have all
"gone glimmering through the realm of things that
were," and oh dear, oh dear ! But I'm not one of
those who say you are simply joking ; oh no. I must
read you until I'm no longer puzzled : you're worth it.

Years ago you said you wanted the theatre to be
"A factory of thought, a prompter of conscience, an
elucidator of social conduct, an armoury against
despair, a temple of the Ascent of Man," and you
have yourself used the theatre consistently for just
those noble ends. Bravo Shaw ! Bravo !

EPILOGUE

By

THE EDITOR

THOMAS PATRICK BARCLAY, Tom Barclay as he was familiarly and affectionately called by his friends, died in his sleep early in the morning on New Year's day 1933, in his eighty-first year. He had never married, and this was a surprise to some of his friends, for he was a lovable man. The explanation is twofold. When in his 'teens he fell in love with a girl, but when he spoke to her he found that her affections were engaged elsewhere. This was a deep and abiding disappointment to him. Then, later, as his understanding developed, and his observation of the facts of life around him made it clear that he was likely to remain poor always, he determined never to marry and beget children to be subject to such horrible privations as those through which he had passed.

That Tom had great affection for his mother is evident enough to anyone who has read the preceding pages. The night of doubt through which he passed before leaving the Catholic Faith was all the more trying for him because he knew that the course he was taking was bound to give pain to his mother, who was a sincere and devout Catholic. Many years afterwards the memory of the distress he had caused her, in doing what he knew was right, filled him with sadness and unavailing regrets. For his sister Kate, his favourite sister, his love was great and enduring. She shared his freethought convictions, and they continued to live together after their mother's death. Later, however, when her health was broken, she made her peace with the Church, and died a Catholic. Then Tom, prompted by his love for her did a finely inconsistent thing. Having no belief whatever in such things himself, he paid for Masses to be said for his sister's soul because Kate would have wished it ! Let who will reproach him for this, I honour and respect him for it.

Here let me tell a story I heard of him many years ago. One night a man who knew him met him on St. Saviour's Road, and was surprised to see that he was crying like a child, He went to him and said "Whatever is the matter Mr. Barclay ? " "Brad-laugh's dead ! " replied Tom. The same deep feeling of affection for one highly prized impelled him, the unbeliever, to pay for Masses for his dead sister, and to shed tears of bitter grief on the death of one who was the champion of the right, and the duty of every man to think freely on all questions, and to hold to the conclusions which seemed to him to be true, against all comers.

That Tom, notwithstanding his affection for his sister, was sometimes rather a trial to her, will not be very surprising to those who had noticed that in some matters he was very unobservant. Many quite ordinary things, observed and acted upon by men very much inferior to him in mental power, he did not observe at all. On one occasion his sister was going away for a day or two, and before going she said, "Now Tom, do try to keep the place tidy whilst I am away." Tom readily promised. So when, on cooking something for himself, he spilt some grease on the grate, and noticed the black shining surface that resulted, he thought that to grease the grate all over was the best way to keep it right. So he greased it all over! No wonder that when Kate returned, and in due course discovered the condition of the grate, and had all the trouble of removing the grease and restoring the normal lustre by means of black lead, some irritation revealed itself when, on relating the incident to a friend, she wound up by saying, "Tom's got every kind of sense, except common sense!"

In matters relating to the condition in which the people about him lived, the ways of the people and their weaknesses, he was an acute and accurate observer. During the period in the nineties when he was working as a bill-distributor, he noted facts and conditions, which he used very effectively in a series of articles in *The Wyvern* on Leicester slums. Here is one, entitled *Where the Poor Live.—Glimpses of Leicester Slums.*"

"In this season of social and political agitation and contention, and while so many public men are discussing the better housing of the people, I offer your readers a little sketch of that slice of Leicester known as Northgate Street. It extends from Sanvey Gate to Frog Island, but is only two hundred yards long: I wish it to be particularly remembered that *it is only two hundred yards long*. Go through, almost any morning from ten to eleven o'clock, and you will see something that ought to be described by a realistic French novelist. At this time the street is very much alive with female forms, working women, who fill the causeways, accosting one another, chatting to one another ; in caps, in hoods, with shawls over their heads, baskets in their hands, and toddling smudge-faced bairns at their apron-strings. They saunter in and out the shops, cheapening and chaffering ; tidy, tattery, slattern, and scant of clothing. Very few though are ragged. Here are three butchers' shops all next door to one another : the cuts are not the prime sort, they look scraggy and bemauled. Shop fronts are dingy, grimy, blackened by friction ; eggs and bacon are seemingly in great demand here ; the glistening kipper too, and the blowsy bloaters—

'Enrich the breeze with their robust perfume,'

and pawnbrokers hang out their clobber on the outward walls. The women continue to pass and re-pass, and one says to himself 'What a teeming population : wherever can they all come from ? ' till suddenly he thinks of the courts. My wonder subsided when I counted from A to R on the right, reckoning from Sanvey Gate, and from T to X on the right, reckoning from Frog Island : eighteen on one side, five on the other—twenty-three in the space of two hundred yards! In the same space there are eight public-houses, three of them with liquor-vaults attached. The brass-barred doors of a couple of these latter being pushed open by mischievous youths as I passed, I beheld groups of women pouring internal libations from small crystal chalices. I supposed them to be engaged in some occult superstitious mystery, but a friend who accompanied me said they were 'only necking the ordinary morning two-penn'orth of rot-gut.' I know not whether 'tis but a small proportion of women who meet thus, or if they meet only on the Monday morn, after the Sunday 'tugs' have been 'shopped' at 'mine uncles' ; ' but this I know, and know full well, that if I lived up one of those courts, in a stuffy, smoky, two-roomed little crib, I might be tempted to go to some kind of anodyne or nepenthe for surcease of sorrow. We can't be too careful in ascertaining whether a desire to drink is the cause of the slum, or whether the slum is the cause of the desire to drink."

The next week he wrote the following—
Leicester Slums.—A Women's Reply and Protest—

"I was a gooin' up Northgate Street that mornin' as you write about in your paper, just to get a bit o' summat for me 'usband's dinner, when I see Misses Smith, pore woman, comin' along, as her 'usband asn't had a bit o' nowt to do ever sin a fortnite arter Bank Holiday. And so Misses Brown as wor along wi' me sez, 'Ow bad Misses Smith does *look* ; she's got summat to go thru, pore wench, ain't she ? And now she's got her least down wi' *Typus*, or summat. Let's tek her in for a drop o' that as'll rouse her up." Well, I've niver bin a grizzle, and so I sez, 'All right : it won't mek us, and it won't brek us.' So we went up to Misses Smith and asked her, but she was that put about, pore thing, that she didn't want to goo. She sed as her Bill 'ud kill her if ever he knowed as she went in a pub. Then Misses

Brown sez, 'O let Bill go and fry his hat ; he goes in
when *he* likes. Come and have a drain to pluck ye
up : it's a pore 'eart as *niver* rejoices.' So we all three
goes into the 'Lord Tom Noddy,' and who should
be there but Misses Jones, the fish-woman, as her
daughter got married only a week or two ago to that
chubby little pork-butcher at the corner. And she
sez, 'Well, we don't meet *every* day, so have one at
my expense. And I'm sure I didn't want, for I wouldn't
thank you for it arter the first glass ; and Misses
Smith sed she dursn't, as it got in her head. However,
we all had one more 'ot, with a little sugar and lemon,
and Misses Jones talked nineteen to the dozen, so
that nodoby could get a word in edgeways. And we
were standin' in the passage, cos we didn't like to
goo and sit down among a lot o' men ; and just then
some lads banged open the door of the passage,
squawking like mad. And I see a man look in, and I
count that's him as is been puttin' us in the *Wyvern*.
But we didn't have nowt at *his* expense, and it's the
only bit of enjoyment as us pore married women gets
now,—that and the mother's meetin'. I count *he*
can goo to the Tivoli and the Opera House, and to
football matches whenever he likes ; but when yer
married ye might as well be buried : it's all up wi'
ye ! I'm a woman as is worked hard all me life every
hour as God sends, and nobody can say black's my
mail ; and so is Misses Smith, and so is Misses Brown,
and so is Misses Jones.

Signed, Mary Robinson.''

Mr. Barclay was interested in men, as men ; their
ideas, their beliefs, their customs, and their condition.

He was no mere nationalist, he was a humanist. Especially was he interested in whatever related to the lives of the masses of ordinary men and women, on whose labour the whole fabric of civilization is built, and who, hitherto, have been so generally excluded from its advantages.

Not only in the busy haunts of men was he observant. His bill-distributing took him occasionally out into the country places—the villages of Leicestershire —and this was to him a welcome change from the sordidness and squalor of city life.   For he was a real lover of nature, and many of his happiest hours were spent amongst the natural beauties of Charnwood Forest.   How observant he was, and with what skill and fine feeling he wrote of the sounds and sights he had noted, let the following three pieces from his pen, printed in the *Wyvern* in the nineties, bear witness—

SUMMER SONG OF THE ELM.

I rise up straightly,
Massive and stately,
My foot in the earth, my head in the sky ;
With multitudinous outspread sheaves
That dip like a cottage's thatch at the eaves,
Enchanting the eye.
And the night-black pits and shadowy rifts,
Between and under my plumy drifts,
Are a mystical joy.

I am city and home to the small feathered people,
Who chime in my mazes like bells in a steeple,
And sweet-breathing kine in the shade of me bide,
When the blaze of my father they may not abide :
For the sun is my father, the earth is my mother,
The streamlet and hill my sister and brother.

I drink the tumultuous heaven-sped rains ;
They turn to the blood of my myriad veins,
Feeding me till I am round and full
As a summer's cloud or a fleece of wool :
Then do I open a hundred arms
To my lover the breeze, of the winsome charms,
And at the dear touch of her petal-soft lips
Tingle and throb to my finger tips.

She sings a song in a murmur small,
Heard like a far-away waterfall ;
She plays a tune : I bow and advance,
And rock my green-crowned head adance,
Nodding and swaying in time to the tune,
All through the space of this bright June.

Happy children we, of the sun,
Mighty father, magical one !
Love we and laugh we till summer is gone.

Spring at Last

"I began to wonder whether there would be any
spring this year ; I knew of course that snowdrops
had been found peeping out at the butt of the walls of
Bradgate ruins as early as February last, that the shy
violets could be discovered in the dykes in March,
and I saw later with my own eyes the pimple-like
burs on the hedges, burs that were to burst into
leaves ; but one swallow does not make a summer, and
two or three indications do not make spring. Later
still I noticed the lanky foal had come to town, and
that everywhere his mother went the foal was sure to
go ; I saw the lambs frisk, springing into the air all
four feet together, and little pigs chasing one another
as if possessed, their ears flapping like rags, while

mother pig with the many pendulous dugs intoned a contented basso-profundo. I got a crick in the neck watching the first skylark as he rose and rose and fluttered, and scattered his rapturous melody from on high ; I observed the eight-petalled buttercups open and wither and cease to be. All these were barbingers and accompaniments of 'the sweet o' the year,' and yet something was wanting ; even apple-blossom blushing from the orchards did not convince me that spring was yet 'ycumen in.' The fact is, the real glory of the season has been delayed—'backwarded,' as country people say—by the abnormal rains and cold winds, and it is not until this twenty-fourth day of May that I recognize the true vernal green on bush and tree and sward.

"To-day I perceive with surprise too that a short week has transformed one season into another ; a week ago there was no hawthorn blossom, and haw-thorn blossom is the crown and cloak of springtide. The buckthorn flower that made scraggy patches in hedges of late was but a sorry reminder of the glorious creamy garb now covering the hedges, drowning the leaves, and wafting the sweetest of all perfumes. To-day the air is filled with light—holds it in solution as it were—and the warmth and moisture of the earth, acted upon by that great magician the sun, are bring-ing forth all the sleeping life of plant and animal to enjoy a span of activity. Amid the bright foliage, the young leaves of the elm are specially enchanting : they always remind me of a shower arrested in mid-air. The laburnum also looks like a shower, but a shower of gold, and the pale purple bunches of the

lilac by the side of it harmonize like the second part
with the 'lead' in a duet. The chestnut has a little
steeple of drab flowers, apparently one to every leaf,
so that the tree looks picked out with flowers like a
peacock's tail with eyes : how very beautiful ! The
meadows are more lovely than they will ever be again
for the rest of the year, for they are lavishly sprinkled
with a blend of yellow buttercups, white daisy, and
pink clover-flower, the combination is delightful.
Bugle, speedwell, forget-me-not, ragged robin, enliven
the road-sides, ladysmocks and cowslips dot the
low-lying places, and bluebells make a haze along the
surface of the woods. The snail comes partly out of
his box, the beetle in complete panoply of armour
hurries across your path, and thousands of midges
perform their bewildering gymnastics. Then the air
is vocal with the songs of birds ; the sparrow and
robin chirp and twitter, rooks croak hoarsely, and
the blackbird sings his plaintive strain undaunted by
the shrilling and piping of his more musical cousin
the throstle, while over the dale is heard a voice as
of an invisible spirit, now coming quite close, now
receding far away ; it is the cuckoo's. His two notes
do not ring sharp, but are breathed softly ; he sings
as though he had velvet in his throat, and the
similarity to a very soft bell swinging is wonderful.
Taking the season all in all, the beautiful colours, the
joyous sounds, the delicious perfumes, the fanning
of warm winds, and the gladdening of the sunlight,
tell me, can the purveyors of the most astonishing
musical and spectacular entertainments produce anything to surpass or equal 'Spring's delights ? ' "

THE WORDS OF THE THRUSH.

"Singers that make sweet music for us all
In our dark hours, as David did for Saul."
Longfellow.

Oh, oh, oh !
I feel, I feel, I feel,
But not woe, Oh no, Oh no,
My heart with joy doth flow, flow, o'erflow, o'erflow, o'erflow.

Like merry bells I peal, I peal, I peal,
Sweet it is, sweet it is, sweet, sweet, Oh sweet !
The beauty of all things round about I greet,
I greet, I greet, I greet, greet, greet ;
I thrill, I gush, I pour myself in joy :
Is it not, is it not, is it not sweetness that never doth cloy ?

It is, Oh it is ; and so I sing, I sing
The Spring, the glory, glory of the Spring.
Flower and tree and sky and brook I sing ;
Them and the love of my lover I sing :
Oh the Spring, the Spring, the Spring, the Spring !

It has been said that any poem should be read aloud, to be properly appreciated. If this little poem be read aloud, briskly and liltingly, as the bird sings, the aptness of its title cannot fail to be felt.

Sociability was an outstanding characteristic in Mr. Barclay. He had a wide circle of friends in various grades of society, and his frequent visits to their homes were immensely enjoyed both by old and young. His talks about books and their authors, and about all manner of social problems and passing events were delightful and informative. His fund of merry humour, of jests, of school-boy "howlers," and of limericks, made many an hour pass quickly and merrily. Sometimes too he had a whistle with him and would delight the youngsters by whistling and dancing Irish jigs. Children grew very fond of him. Twenty years ago, when my own two children were quite little, he called one day to see me, but I was out ; after some talk with my wife and the children he rose to go, but the children got hold of him, each holding one leg, and pleaded "Don't go Mr. Barclay, don't go !" His sociability also frequently took him into taverns, or clubs, where he was likely to meet with congenial spirits—men who cared for the things of the mind. And in such company, whilst he was sometimes a learner, and always alert to learn, he was usually the teacher to whose informed discourse the others listened with delight. Since Tom's death, one who is now the active head of a considerable business in Leicester and Hull has talked to me about the very great profit and delight he and a little group of other young men used to get, twenty or thirty years ago, whenever they could induce Tom Barclay to come to their group and talk to them about some of the books he had read, about the problems the books dealt with, about the authors, about the workings of the human mind, and about future social developments. And not only did he thus associate with those whom he knew to be kindred spirits. Just as he was constantly on the look-out for new authors of worth, so he was continually seeking to find new friends from whom to learn, and with whom to share the treasures of his mind. In public houses that he visited, in the public libraries, on the Parks, in the streets of the city or the lanes of the countryside he was anxious to find men who were *thinking*, from whom he could receive, or to whom he could give light and help, and with whom he could find fellowship.   Sometimes he succeeded—and also sometimes he failed.   Let me give one instance of each.   Whilst walking alone, in Anstey Lane, he got into conversation with a stranger, and soon found he had intellectual interests ; knew something about psychology, and discussed *Back to Methuselah* with interest and understanding.   Though I cannot discover that Tom ever saw him again he had enjoyed at least one hour of fellowship with a kindred spirit.   On another occasion having been out rambling alone, Tom called at the Talbot Inn, Belgrave, for refreshment, and found several men sitting there in conversation.   Presently he heard the word psychology mentioned.   This interested him at once, and approaching the group he said to the man who had used the word, "Do you know anything about Psychology ? "   "I should think I do ! " said the man, "I backed the blighter ! "

Tom's great sociability, combined with equally characteristic generosity and guilelessness, made him from time to time an easy victim for spongers, and some of his friends occasionally intervened before things had gone far.   But one man, in a good position, with an annual salary far higher than Tom had ever any hopes of getting, with the prospect of a good pension on retirement, fastened on to Tom and got several pounds out of him before any of Tom's friends knew what was happening.   When they did find out they quickly stopped that little game, and were not surprised when shortly afterwards the man was brought before the magistrates and sent to prison for shameful neglect of his wife and children.

But the guilelessness which made him such an easy prey did on one occasion serve him in good stead. It was on this wise. The Socialist propagandists of the early days followed the practice at their open-air meetings of appealing for a quiet hearing for their speakers, and promising, if this were given, that at the close of the address opportunity would be given to anyone in the audience not only to ask questions but also to come on to the platform and put forward any opposing view. Mr. Barclay was addressing a meeting from a lorry in Humberstone Gate on one occasion, and had an audience of about a couple of hundred people, when up came two policemen, a sergeant and a constable, intending to stop the meeting. The sergeant forced his way through the crowd, and when he got right up to the platform he spoke to Tom and told him to stop. Tom, regarding him as an ordinary interrupter said to him "I am addressing this audience, and you must not interrupt ; anything you have to say you may say when I have finished," and immediately proceeded with his address. The sergeant was taken aback, and didn't know what to do. However, in a few minutes he again spoke to Tom and said that he must not continue. Tom again turned to the sergeant and, whilst he was still quite courteous, he was a little more explicit. "Now sergeant," he said, "I told you before you must not interrupt me whilst I am addressing this audience. If only you will wait till I have finished you are quite welcome to come on this platform and say whatever you wish to say." The crowd laughed and cheered, Tom continued and finished his speech, and the sergeant retired quite discomfited by Tom's *naivete*.

A physical idiosyncrasy from which Mr. Barclay suffered—inability to perspire—used to cause him a good deal of discomfort in hot weather. The relief from excessive heat which perspiration provides being denied him, he was driven to seek relief in such ways as he could. Long before the cult of hatlessness started he would be seen walking through the streets reading a paper or a book, with hat or cap tucked under his arm, regardless of the amusement of the more thoughtless or conventional of the passers-by. To secure ease in his feet, whether from constriction or from heat he would cut half a dozen slits in the uppers of his boots. When walking in the country he would be as likely as not to take off his boots and stockings and trudge along in bare feet carrying the discarded footwear under his arm. Sometimes groups of young people passing him laughed at this proceeding, and their laughter mystified Tom, for there was nothing to laugh at in such sensible conduct. One one occasion he went for a ramble in the country with two of his friends—Fred Hollis and Alf. Tebb—and as the afternoon advanced, and they became both tired and hot with their walk, they tried at a little shop, in a village through which they were passing, to get a cup of tea. This the shopkeeper was unable to supply. Would they have some ice-cream ? Yes, failing tea, they would. Each was supplied with a portion in a saucer, together with a spoon with which to eat it. Tom tried a spoonful, didn't like it, and spat it out. This was too much for

the friends who promptly turned their backs upon
him. By-and-by, wondering what else he might be
doing they looked round and saw that he was putting
the ice-cream on the top of his head to give him
relief from the burning heat ; and he was utterly
surprised when he found that they did not regard
this proceeding with complete approval ! It was Fred
Hollis with whom Tom on one occasion was discussing the question of the permanence, or otherwise, of
the novel as a literary form. Fred contended that
Fiction was merely a temporary vogue, and said that
F. J. Gould (at that time Secretary of the Leicester
Secular Society) held that opinion. "Oh," said Tom,
"and what does he think will take its place ? "
"Biography," replied Hollis. Tom laughed, and said
"Biography ?   That will mean more fiction than
ever ! "

   It was an abiding trial to Tom that so many working
men took not the slightest interest in books, in
politics, in economics, in social questions, in music
or any form of art, but were wholly engrossed in
sport, in gambling, in drink. To be in close association during the whole of the working day with those
incapable of interest, or unwilling to attempt to
become interested, in the things which to him were
of the highest importance, was like being deprived of
freedom and fresh air. Many an attempt did he make
to show them how these things would enrich their
lives, but in most cases without success. Some did
respond and gladly availed themselves of his guidance
in their first efforts to find their way in the world of
books, and they bless him for the good they have

gained.   Others resented Tom's reproaches, and attempted to make fun of him because of his fondness for books, and then Tom would take an impish delight in mystifying them by speaking bookish language about common things, and by using many syllabled words to indicate what they were to do, as when he said they must "remove the coagulated sedimentary deposit" from the bottles they had to wash. The effect of this on their minds was shown one day when one of the men who was reading a newspaper and had come across a couple of words he could not read, asked Tom what the words were. Tom looked at the paper and read them to him, "bacteriological therapeutics," at the same time explaining briefly what they meant. The man looked again at the paper, and slowly and painfully uttered the words.   He then looked up and said "Why, God's truth Tom, I always thought you made them up, but there they are !" Another man, who thought to quiz Tom about his reading, asked him one day "And what are you reading now Tom ? "   Tom knew his man, and, pausing a moment before answering, reduced him to silence by saying, slowly and impressively, "At the present time I am reading two tremendous tomes on an esoteric subject called comparative anthropology ! "

The period of Mr. Barclay's greatest intellectual and political activity was during the eighties and the nineties, and for a few years at the beginning of the present century.   Then, gradually, and inevitably, advancing years and the hard life he had always led produced increasing weakness and weariness, for he

still had to maintain himself by labouring work of
one kind or another,* and his activities necessarily
declined. But the old spirit was there still, and continued to the end. These were the years when Ireland
was passing through such troublous times, and two
surviving scraps from an old diary will show how
these things distressed him. The first is an entry in
July 1919, when the "Black-and-Tans" were harrying
Ireland so shamefully.

"I thank whatever Gods may be that if I couldn't
be great I could appraise and love and reverence
greatness.

> Fail I alone in words and deeds ?
> Why all men strive, and who succeeds ?

Let it go on record though, if some friend who knew
me should come across these wild notes,—if they
should come into the hands of someone I liked such
as George or James Kelly, or Owen Lochran, or
Gorrie, or Charley Crisp,—or—or Bernard Shaw
himself, or Dom Macarthy, that I—*moi qui parle*,
Tom Barclay, wanted to *do* something—within three
days of being sixty-seven wanted to *do* something—
for poor, distracted, ill-fated Ireland ! What can I
do ? I am nobody, nothing—no means ! ! ! Peace, be
still ! If you had a million you could do nothing now
but dream and give your money to the cause—I
would too."

The second relates to the period of internecine
conflict in Ireland after the making of the Treaty.

"Beginning to be ashamed and disgusted with

* During the last twenty-five years his work was mainly that
of a bottle-washer.

PROTEST OF AN IRISHMAN IN
LEICESTER
To The Editor.

Sir,— Will you kindly allow me as a man – as an Irishman especially—to take up a brief space on the murders, the cowardly and brutal murders, in Ireland of Mr. Burke and Lord F. Cavendish. I know I shall not be expressing my own feelings merely, but those also of my Irish fellow-townsmen, when I say that the cold-blooded assassination of the new Irish Chief Secretary can only be regarded with the greatest abhorrence. There have been many and deplorable crimes attending the Irish agitation since its commencement. But they have for the most part been enveloped in such a fog of landlord oppression, self- protection, and personal recrimination as to make it difficult to take the exact measure of their heinousness; but the present murder is of such a character as to make Irishmen hang down their heads. But the ruffians who have taken away the life of the unfortunate Lord Cavendish have, it is to be feared done an incalculable amount of injury besides. They have created a prejudice against Irishmen and the Irish cause that will not be easily dissipated. Just at the time, too, when the Government had agreed to abandon the policy of coercion; when the prisons were flung open, when the arrears were to be dealt with and who knows what large and generous measures besides?

The Government had agreed to consult with the responsible Irish leaders. Poor Ireland had begun to think she had got at the "beginning of the end," when—alas ! all this will be reversed, perhaps, by the inhuman act of some wretch or wretches who thus cruelly murder an unoffending stranger, an untried and unknown gentleman, and at the same time destroy the hopes of a whole people.

But, sir, this is no agrarian crime ; and the people I am sure will aid the law in stamping out this terrible state of things. Whoever the dastards be I sincerely trust they will be speedily discovered and brought to justice.—Yours Truly,

THOMAS BARCLAY.

20 , Argyle•street, Leicester.

————————◆————————

From *The LeicesterChronicle and Mercury,* 20th. May 1882

Barclay spoke for the Irish in Leicester in expressing his deep dismay with the Phoenix Park murders; nonetheless, a close reading of the letter gives an indication of his acute political awareness of the delicacy, then as now, involved in Anglo-Irish relations

Death Of Tom Barclay

FRIEND OF

RUSKIN AND SHAW

Many of the older generation of Leicester politicians and students will mourn the passing of Tom Barclay, who died in hospital yesterday at the age of 80.

He was in humble circumstances all his life, yet he had more influence upon the city's intellectual life than most of those in high stations.

He was an Irishman—and proud of it—and his family came to Leicester not long after the famine years—1846 and 1847.

Fine French Scholar

Not much education was obtainable by poor people in his young days without hard struggle, but young Tom learned from everything and everybody, and his knowledge of literary matters was deep and wide. Incidentally, he read French almost as well as English.

Ruskin, and later Bernard Shaw, were his literary gods, and he became personally acquainted with both of them. The former was strongly against any publication of selections from his works, but Tom Barclay succeeded in getting his consent to the publication of an interesting collection of quotations which had a good sale.

With Shaw, Tom conducted many an argument, and he was the proud possessor of several characteristic G.B.S. communications beginning with "Dear Tom."

A convinced Socialist, Tom Barclay threw himself into the Fabian Branch of the movement, and when the famous Fabian Lectures were delivered in Leicester he reported them for William Morris's weekly "The Commonwealth."

Always a man who was fond of an argument, and a fighting spirit at heart, Tom Barclay mellowed as he grew older, but his Irish disposition kept him a keen critic as well as an optimist. He was one of the oldest members of the Leicester Secular Society, to which he belonged before the hall was opened in 1881.

From the *LeicesterMercury* 2nd. January, 1933. (p.15)

Barclay's obituary notice in the local paper encompasses the dichotomy he represented; a private, self-effacing man, yet one who had had a profound influence on the city where he spent his life.

things Irish.   Killing one another ! Treatyite, Republican, Orangeman, phut !   Shades of Michael Davitt, Emmett, Tone, O'Connell, MacSweeney, Connolly, Orr, Tandy, Mitchell, Parnell, Davis, Smith O'Brien, Redmond, Sarsfield, Red Hugh, Pearse, O'Meagher, Duffy — O woe is me, my torment ! Factions, reactions, distractions and . . . and finally—Fractions ! "

During all those unhappy years his distress at the course things were taking in Ireland was all the greater because he was so powerless to do anything effective to help the country to which he was attached by strong sentiment.

There came a time at last when he could no longer read a book through, though he still dipped into books of various kinds. Then his friend Fred Hollis said to him "Why bother about reading more books now Tom ; you have got plenty in your own noddle. Why not write your own memoirs ? There is a big enough field for you there to keep you occupied and interested."   The suggestion was a happy one, and Tom acted upon it, and it is from what he wrote, in what he called his *Memoirs and Medleys*, that the preceding chapters have been compiled. When at last he ceased work, and lived on his old age pension, eked out by the little he had saved from his meagre earnings, this writing was a real boon to him, keeping him happily occupied, when without it he might have endured great boredom. And after a time he seemed to get rested in body and mind. His appetite for books returned and he again read widely books of many kinds. But his favourite author was still Bernard Shaw, and he read again with immense relish the earlier plays which he had not read for years, and turned to the *Metabiological Pentateuch* determined to stick to it until he could understand all that Shaw was driving at in that marvellous series. He talked with individual friends, and even chance acquaintances about it, and discussed with them the possibility of forming a Shaw Society. He went to various groups and gave addresses on Shaw and his works, and during the last few weeks of his life he was gathering notes "for an address—or a *book*—on Shaw's biographers," reading the works of such as he had not already become familar with, in the process. In his diary only a week before he died is a note of one such book, the last of a long series extending over several months. To the end he wanted to *do* something !

Did Mr. Barclay, like his sister Kate, return to the Catholic Faith before he died ? The question has been put to me by more persons than one ; so lest any uncertainty should exist on this point it had better be answered here, simply and categorically. He did not. Evidence of his continuance as a freethinker is plentiful in his latest writings. After his death his niece, herself a Catholic, told me that when his last illness came on she asked him would he like to see a priest, and he said "No. It would be no good. I know more than he knows !" In his *Memoirs and Medleys*, very near the end, is an extract from the diary of Marie Bashkirtseff :—"Though there be no God to hear my evening prayer, yet I pray to Him every night in despite of my reason." He adds this comment, "Poor Marie, you're a psychological puzzle like so many more of us. Thought and feeling are at variance within you. You *wish* there were a God—a close worthy friend and counsellor to love, reverence, confide in. Millions of us down the ages have wished the same. Hence totems, fetishes, apparitions, prayers, miracles, inspirations, consecrations, Holy Scriptures, commandments, benedictions, and excommunications." In Tom also "thought and feeling" were "at variance." But he maintained his intellectual integrity to the end. He faced the end quite contentedly, as this further extract from his *Medleys* foreshadowed.

> "Into the breast that gives the rose
> Shall I with shuddering fall ? "

Tom's sufficient comment was "I, for one, hope not !"

That Tom Barclay was a remarkable man is evident enough from the narrative he has himself set down. To say that he had weaknesses, foibles, defects, is only to say that he was human. Some of these weaknesses only made him the more lovable. But the really outstanding qualities which characterized him—his insatiable thirst for knowledge, his determined and unremitting efforts to obtain it, his intellectual integrity, his disregard of convention and his courageous following his own course, his consideration for the feelings and interests of other people, his modesty, his innate courtesy, his utter lack of self-seeking and his whole-hearted devotion to social welfare—these are the qualities which commanded the admiration, respect and affection of those whose privilege it was to be intimately acquainted with him, and were capable of appreciating them. He was a rebel against the existing social and economic order. This should surprise no one who knew the background of his life——the surprising thing was the utter lack of rancour and bitterness which marked his advocacy of revolutionary change. There was always marked courtesy in his dealing with opponents —never an attempt to make them look foolish, always an effort by sweet reasonableness to win them to his view. He was *really* a *free*-thinker. He detested bigotry, and he respected those who held opinions he did not agree with, whenever he believed those opinions had been freely formed, and were sincerely held. He was always more glad to give than to receive. to serve other people than to be served by them. Some men by their lives tend to destroy belief in human worth. It is the crowning glory of such a man as Tom Barclay that intimacy with him created, confirmed and increased faith in the essential goodness of human nature.

James K. Kelly.